Great styles of furniture

Great

English

Italian

French

Dutch

Spanish

styles of furniture

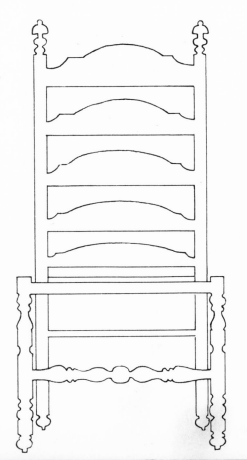

A STUDIO BOOK

The Viking Press · New York

© LE RAYONNEMENT FRANÇAIS
PUBLISHED IN 1963 BY THE VIKING PRESS, INC.
625 MADISON AVENUE, NEW YORK 22, N.Y.
LIBRARY OF CONGRESS CATALOG CARD NUMBER: 63-18910
PRINTED IN FRANCE BY LES IMPRIMERIES DE BOBIGNY

Contents

Italy

France

Holland

Spain

Chronological Table of Furniture Styles

The illustrations in this book are reproduced by kind permission of the following museums and collections

ENGLAND: The Royal Collection, by gracious permission of Her Majesty the Queen; the National Trust; the Victoria and Albert Museum, London.

ITALY: Museo Poldi Pezzoli and Castello Sforzesco, Milan; Cà Rezzonico, Venice.

FRANCE: Palace of Versailles; Musée des Arts Décoratifs, Paris.

HOLLAND: Rijksmuseum and Municipal Museum, Amsterdam; Centraal Museum, Utrecht; Municipal Museum, The Hague; Netherlands Open-Air Museum, Arnhem; Museum of the Castle of Popta, Maarsum; Paul Tetar van Elven Museum, Delft.

SPAIN: Museo Nacional de Artes Decorativas and Museo Romántico, Madrid.

In addition, the publishers are indebted to the private individuals and collectors who allowed them to reproduce pieces from their collections, or to photograph their homes.

The photographs are by

Adrion; Claude Basnier; Gisèle de la Begassière; Boudot-Lamotte; Franck Beyda; André Chadefaux; Patrice Clement; Dominique Darbois; Augustin Dumage; R. Gauthier; Giraudon; Pierre Hommet; Pierre Jahan; Musée des Arts Decoratifs; Editions Plaisir de France; Génia Rubin; Rys Dorvyne; Marie-Loup Sougez; Marc Vaux.

Introduction

As wealth and security, and with them some greater ease and graciousness of life became more general in the 15th century, furniture and the furnishing of the home began to play an important part in the background of daily life, not only for the very rich but for quite a large section of the people. The simple benches and trestles, beds and coffers that had hitherto served their basic utilitarian purpose became the vehicle for decoration and ornament. Morally, it might be more respectable if we could claim that this development arose purely on aesthetic grounds, or even from a search for greater cleanliness and comfort. But, although these elements may have been present, it would be foolish to pretend that the desire for display and status was not more influential. Certainly it was very important in promoting the succeeding changes of style, which came and went as do fashions in other arts and crafts, or even clothes, and for the same reasons. It is with these changes that this volume is concerned.

The basic furniture designs have always been common to the whole of Europe, and particular forms and ornament seem to follow the main stream of artistic development. Thus Italian and Italianate conceptions dominate at the Renaissance, while French influences are marked in the early 18th century and English at the end.

The time lag in the adoption or adaptation of certain styles was often fairly considerable, and this applies as much within the individual countries as internationally. Manifestly people did not go to the expense and bother of refurnishing at the speed and frequency with which they renewed their clothes. Besides, such trades as joinery or cabinet making were not often geared to rapid change. An apprentice trained in his youth to work in a certain way was likely to continue to do so all his working life, so that in the provinces—especially in the country—a style some decades out of the latest metropolitan fashion might well be current. The same, indeed, occurs today when despite all the encouragement to keep in advance, designs of the 1920's and even earlier still obtain.

Against the background, certain basic forms came and went, those best adapted to practical needs lasting longest. In this way a piece like the fall front desk appears all over Europe, and is virtually the same whether it is called the bargueño in Renaissance Spain, or in its latest form on a chest of drawers, the 'secretaire abattant' in 18th-19th

9

century France. The chest of drawers itself, in one form or another, has never lapsed since its introduction. Similarly, certain easy effects like the 'barley sugar twist' for chair legs travelled almost everywhere and lasted for several generations.

To these forms and designs regional traditions added their own effects. Sometimes these alter shape or size, at other times merely influence the decoration by inlay or mouldings, pokerwork or marquetry according to some local craft or fancy.

These regional deviations are perhaps more marked in the case of furniture than in other arts or crafts. Once the idea of furnishing had grown up, everyone wanted beds and cupboards, chairs or tables, of a greater or lesser degree of elaboration. As furniture, at least ordinary furniture, was not expensive, quite modest people could aspire to some pretension in their homes. But as furniture is bulky and transport expensive, all but the very rich tended to buy locally-made pieces rather than to import. All these factors combined to allow greater freedom of expression to local craftsmanship and taste. Again, since the furniture had to go into houses, its design was bound to be influenced in some degree by regional architecture, if only to the extent that large pieces were better suited to large rooms, and so on. Local materials also assumed considerable importance in the demands they made or the opportunities they afforded. Indeed the main early stylistic division as between northern France, the Low Countries and England, as opposed to southern France or Spain and Italy, probably owed something to the general use of oak in the north and walnut in the south. Italian designs basically created for walnut adopted curious modifications when interpreted in the oak of Flanders or England. But these, as also all the other period styles, are better studied in the individual sections which follow.

What may chiefly concern us in this Introduction is how the major influences spread.

The answer seems to be three-fold. Pattern books, the movement of craftsmen themselves and lastly the movement of actual pieces of furniture.

At any time with which we are concerned the printed books of patterns and designs were available and were extensively used in all countries. For especial pieces for the Court or particular Commissions artists drew designs, but for the great mass of work the printed sheets and books sufficed. At first these were mainly Italian or French, or northern copies and adaptations. By the early 18th century the French predominate, and later, English examples enjoyed great vogue. The designs for rooms and individual pieces or for simple ornament by artists like du Cerceau or Marot or Pineau were immensely influential, and there were many others. The earlier English works, often copied from Flemish or French designs, were used chiefly at home, but with the publication of Chippendale's *Director* and the engraved works of Robert Adam, Hepplewhite and Sheraton later in the 18th century, the English influence spread all over Europe.

The movement of artisans had considerable effect both within their own countries and abroad. The traffic, for example, between northern Europe and England had been active during the Middle Ages and continued throughout the 16th, 17th and 18th centuries. After the religious persecutions in France many Huguenot refugees came to London. Usually these craftsmen seem to have been welcome but sometimes there were difficulties, as when a northern Guild petitioned against German immigrants. Sometimes craftsmen of high quality travelled to seek a wider outlet for their abilities than could be found at home. A notable example is to be found in the movement of German inlay workers and craftsmen at various times, but at none more spectacularly than in Paris in the 18th century. Oeben, Weisweiller or Roentgen, to name but three, were all of German origin, but made their name and established their world-famous businesses in Paris. Obviously this city offered a far better outlet than their small home towns. But there must have been other reasons for movement; as was perfectly natural, the more gifted or the more ambitious apprentices sought to find their training at the most important centres. Just as naturally, not all of them could find a future there, so that once they had obtained their mastership they travelled wherever they thought they might do best for themselves. Sometimes this was abroad, as is instanced by the great influx of foreign craftsmen into America, though more usually these people migrated to provincial centres in their own country. Thus we find that in 18th-century provincial England almost all local advertisements proclaimed London contacts or London training. There is, of course, the other side of the medal. At later periods when more important people tended to buy everything from the metropolis and put up with the expenses of transport, the outlet for the very best workmen was at the big centres, so that we may suspect that many of those who came away were artisans of second-rate talent, or those who were not ready to accept subordinate positions in a larger workshop and sought to establish themselves where there was less competition. This was obviously not always the case, since family ties or the inheritance of a business might keep a man away from London or Paris, but it no doubt accounts in part for the "provincial" qualities of much provincial furniture.

Lastly, there was the movement of actual pieces themselves. Here the influence on the craft itself is perhaps less easy to assess, either nationally or internationally, since the difficulty of moving furniture normally meant that only the best pieces needed for the best houses were likely to travel. At the same time these pieces must have provided some stimulus and example.

Internationally, we know that throughout the whole of the period, persons of the highest fashion imported finished pieces as well as foreign craftsmen. In the 16th century examples of elaborate inlay or Flemish cabinets were popular. Oriental exotica were always sought after. So much so, that by the end of the 17th century the importation of oriental lacquer had everywhere assumed importance as a business. This continued right throughout the 18th century, extending to textiles and even wallpapers as the Eastern trade developed. There were several collections of fine 18th-century French furniture in England and Germany, and even in Russia. Later, English pieces travelled to the Continent as well as to America. These are but examples of an activity that seems to have been fairly universal.

Until recent times the whole idea of frequent change in home decoration and furniture was rare, except perhaps in 18th-century France or among the very rich and fashionable. Houses were furnished and decorated at the time of building, re-done perhaps on inheritance or purchase or the owner's marriage, and in the vast majority of cases done with the best and most solid that the money available could buy. The owner's intention was usually that these furnishings should last his lifetime and those of his children's children too. Occasionally, for reasons of family sentiment or from indifference or lack of money such settings have remained intact. Sometimes this preservation has been helped by the fact that the 'best rooms' were rarely used. But such untouched rooms are rare, houses were sold, families died out, new generations wanted new fashions and new furniture was acquired. Fortunately many of the individual pieces have remained. Good quality, well-made furniture is fairly indestructible, and even if the pieces passed from the state rooms to the attics, they still remained repairable if not intact. There was always a second-hand market for fine furniture and, as the trade cards show, few cabinet makers were above part exchange.

So it is that a great many pieces have passed down to us as serviceable and beautiful as when they were made. This book tells us something of their story, and how they can be set about for use today.

CHARLES VANDAM

ENGLAND

Frontispiece. *A Room in Buckingham House* by Johann Zoffany (1733-1810). The two children are probably the Prince of Wales and the Duke of York. Royal Collection, Windsor.

Introduction

To judge from such few pieces as remain, furniture and furnishing in England during the Middle Ages, like the other arts, followed the general lines which prevailed over the rest of Europe, and could certainly claim parity in quality and execution. But after the 14th century the unending wars and religious or political upheavals scarcely created a background to maintain the country in the vanguard of advancing taste.

Thus medieval traditions persisted long after the establishment of the Tudor monarchy, and it was not until well into the 16th century that Renaissance influences came to dominate form and design. Even then, the Italian elements appeared in a somewhat provincial interpretation, developed largely through craftsmen or patterns from the Low Countries. Baroque influences, such as they were, came after the Restoration of Charles II in 1660, and it was not until the advent of greater security and wealth by the 18th century that English artistic genius could re-establish itself, and finally, by the end of the century, play a leading rôle.

As far as it can be said that there are any essentially English characteristics, they are perhaps more clearly defined at this later period. A taste for simplicity and even severity of form and line, coupled with a feeling for proportion and for material, is perhaps the keynote of this English quality. With this reticence in design there has also been a tendency to fairly restricted scale. English rooms at any period are generally smaller than those on the Continent and the furniture corresponds.

As elsewhere, a practice has grown up by which styles are identified by the names of reigning monarchs. Though practical, this can be misleading if too exactly pursued, as no style directly responds to so precise a dating, and few developments in England owe much to the personal intervention of the sovereigns. Furthermore, though the island is small so that regional variations are limited, a time lag seems always to have existed as between London and the provinces, no doubt encouraged by a certain innate conservatism in the English character. Thus an exact dating on stylistic grounds is unwise in default of ancillary evidence.

CHARLES VANDAM

Tudor

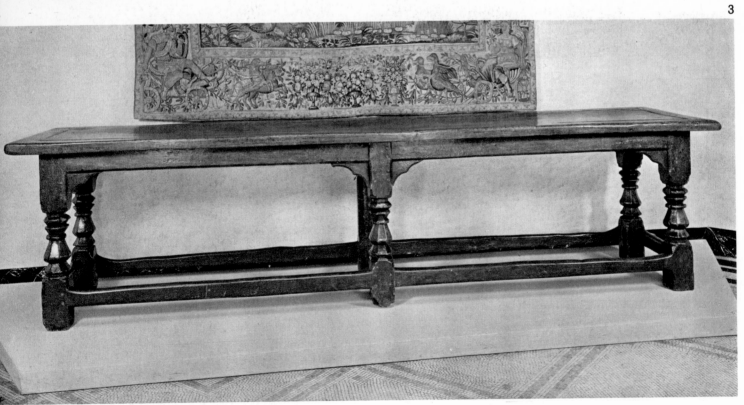

4

2, 4. Panelled construction and linenfold decoration served not only for screens and wainscotting (panelling), but also for coffers and chests, chairs and tables.

5. This leather-covered chest with Tudor arms conforms to a general type of European table-desk enclosing numerous drawers, like the Spanish bargueño. These desks had the advantage of being readily transportable, and it is probable that examples such as this may have been used rather in the Royal service than for the King himself.

6. In the case of this later, smaller example, with its elaborate painted decoration, a more immediate service of the King is implied. The painting of arms—in this case those of Henry VIII—and the general style suggests foreign workmanship and a date well into the 16th century. It is redolent of the more elaborate decorative developments of colour, silver, tapestries, to the taste of contemporary monarchy. Such pieces were, however, fairly rare, and limited to the highest in the land.

Simple, useful oak furniture and late Gothic design persisted well into the 16th century under the Tudors. Occasional carving—usually foliage, simple geometrical designs or 'linenfold' panels—provided the basis of ornament. These simple designs are well represented by the solid table (3). The Giffard Screen (1) provides an example of more elaborate furniture decoration.

5   6

1. This bed illustrates the developments well established among English workers by the second half of the 16th century. The profusion of ornament on the back is typical, with its caryatids, carved geometrical ornament, arcading, foliage work and grotesques, and so are the column supports with the big balusters. Though Italianate in origin, the interpretation is entirely northern, and owes much to Flemish influence and pattern books. The overall effect is rich, but the detail of the craftsmanship is still rather coarse.

1

Elizabethan

2

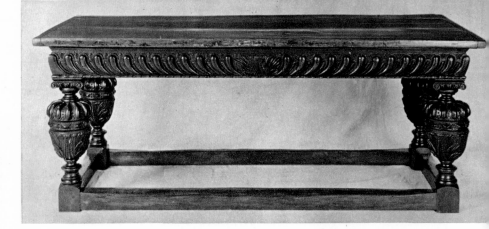

2, 3. The same features appear on this typical 'Court cupboard' and table. Drawtops were often to be found at this period, though they have sometimes been replaced in the 19th-century romantic revival of Elizabethan taste, or later.

3

Opposite page: This room with its early type of panelling, inset romantic historical series of pictures, plaster ceiling and mixed furniture is typical of a 20th-century English taste for restoring historic houses. Usually this is done with some care for period architecturally, but with a pleasant 'homely' confusion in the individual furnishing pieces. The 'Tudor' styles were especially popular between the wars; later taste has tended to turn to the 18th century.

The 17th Century

Despite commissions by Charles I to Rubens and Bernini, the general taste under that King was towards more severity, as under James I before him and the Commonwealth which followed.

1. This panelled room, reputedly from Houghton House and thus associable with Bunyan, the notable 'blue stocking' Countess of Pembroke, sister of Philip Sidney, and even Inigo Jones, expresses the essence of the reaction against Elizabethan High Renaissance. The extreme classical severity of the conception, adapted straight from Vitruvius, is heightened by the Latin verse over the mantelpiece. This is concerned, like much thought of the day, with death and the hereafter. Such preoccupations were unlikely to produce lively furnishing, and though this is perhaps an extreme example, it underlines the general trend.

1

Turned ornament, as in the first of the two chairs on the right (2), is characteristic of the Low Countries. It became popular in England in the 17th century, as elsewhere on the Continent, and persisted for some time.

Like the Houghton Room, the second chair on the right (3), said to have belonged to Archbishop Juxon, is notable for its severity and for its 'classical' design.

Something of the approaching severity is manifest even in this transitional bed (5). This is readily seen if we compare it with the example on the previous page. It follows the earlier style in its general form and armorial bearings, but is far more restrained in the other decorations. The same characteristics mark the stools and table (4).

2 3

4 5

Restoration

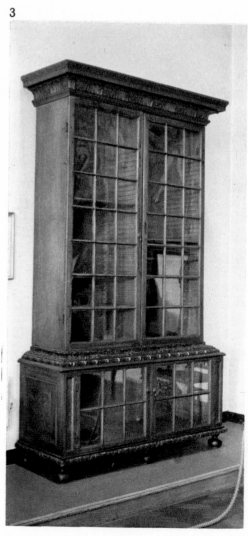

English furniture at the Restoration of Charles II (1660) emphasizes the revolt against Puritan severity, and leans towards elaborate decoration influenced by Continental Baroque. Lacquer cabinets on elaborate stands (1), either imported or 'Japanned' at home, became extremely popular. Indeed, the fashion for Japanning became such that a treatise on it was produced in the 1680's by Stalker and Parker, addressed to amateurs among the quality as well as the trade. This period also saw the heyday of the elaborately carved swags of fruit and flowers (2) associated with the name of Grinling Gibbons. Carved decoration also returned to favour. The highback chair (4) and simpler bookcase (3) are fine examples. The chest of drawers (5) is transitional with simple lines in the William and Mary style. The geometric mouldings and panelling of (6), taken from the Low Countries, were still used for more ordinary pieces.

William and Mary

The last quarter of the century saw a swing back again towards simplicity under Dutch influence. This change was no doubt accelerated by the accession of William of Orange as William III.

Tasteful proportions and an appreciation for fine woods and veneers were the foundation of this style, and these criteria persisted right through the great flowering of English cabinet making during the 18th century. This 'scriptor' from Ham House offers a beautiful example. It appears in an inventory as early as 1679.

1

2

3

1, 2. Both these cabinets show developments of the same basic idea (see previous page, Ham House scriptor). In these pieces the elaborate marquetry of coloured woods and ivory, probably again influenced by Dutch designers, provided an opportunity for those who still liked something of the richness of Restoration ornamental furniture.

3, 4, 5. The seat (3) with its contemporary upholstery, as also the stool (4) and table (5), again emphasizes Dutch design and the movement to simpler forms in plain wood. The ornament in all three pieces rests largely on the shaped feet and stretchers.

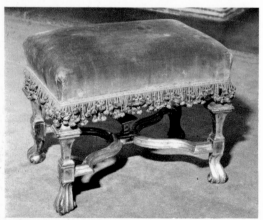

4

5

Queen Anne

The advent of the 18th century saw further refinements towards simplicity, and a dependence on line and material rather than on carving or applied ornament. The favourite material was walnut.

The pieces on this page are typical of the style popularly known as Queen Anne, though it persisted long after the end of her reign in 1714, and had begun earlier.

1, 2, 3, 5. Proportion and a respect for the fine walnut veneers are the significant features of these pieces.

4. The card table with its variegated laburnum top represents a more elaborate taste.

1

2

3

4

5

1

2

Georgian

Furniture at the beginning of the Hanoverian period was in essence a slightly elaborated Queen Anne, as we see in this chair (1) and double settee (2), dating from the second or even third decade of the century. Though line and wood provide the decorative elements, the former flows a little more sinuously, and the latter is enhanced by very discreet carved shell motifs, and, in the case of the seat, the carved 'claw and ball' feet which are so marked a feature of Georgian furniture.

As examples of the persistence of traditional elaborate taste, the gilt gesso table below (3), dating from about 1715, really carries on the decorative ideas of about 1700, while the candle stand (4) combines earlier motifs with a more severely classical form.

3

4

5

6

7　8

The establishment in power of the aristocratic Whig party under the first Hanoverians (George I and II) brought a return of greater opulence and splendour, to provide for the great country palaces being built. This style was prevented from assuming all the exotic elaboration of Continental Rococo by the influence of the classical 'Palladian' group, led by Lord Burlington and others. The name of the artist William Kent is popularly associated with the period. Architectural features were fashionable, as in the swags and broken pediment of the bureau-bookcase (7), and, slightly more elaborate and less classically formal, in the chair with gilt enrichments (5) and mirror of gilded wood (6). The table (8), based on a French design by Pineau, represents a concession to Continental Rococo. It also marks the increasingly important part to be played by mahogany in English mid-18th-century furniture.

27

Thomas Chippendale

The Gentleman's and Cabinet Maker's Director

In 1753 the firm of Thomas Chippendale brought out an elaborate design book, which quickly ran into three editions and was undoubtedly influential on design both at home and abroad.

These designs from Chippendale's *Director* show above all the eclecticism of his production which ranges from the severe, simple, traditional English designs, in which the merits of the object still depend upon proportion and wood —now normally mahogany—to others in which every variety of line and ornament are pressed into service.

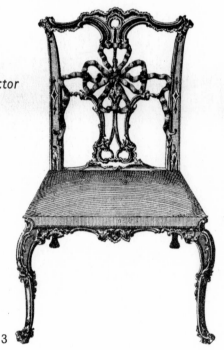

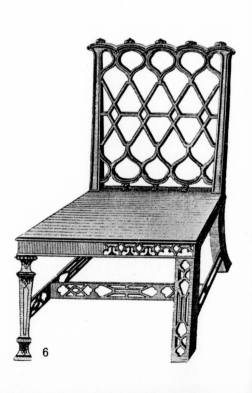

The later 18th Century

At the mid-century a revolutionary change came over English furniture. This concerned not only fashionable styles, but the organization of the trade itself. At least in London and the larger towns, the individual cabinet makers gave place to larger firms employing many workmen, prepared to undertake the complete furnishing and decoration of the home.

The high esteem in which design books by Chippendale, Hepplewhite and Sheraton were held led to those furniture styles which followed the general design in their volumes being known by their names. Yet while the Chippendales were a successful and active firm, they were only one of many. No documented example by Hepplewhite exists, and we do not know for certain whether Sheraton worked as a cabinet maker at all— at least at the date of his books.

The pieces here are typical of the period. The simple bookcase (2) and slightly more elaborate commode (3) in the French taste lead up to the very elaborate carved mirror, for which the design (by Mathias Locke, who worked for Chippendale) still exists.

1

2

3

4

On this page we find a group of chairs of the more carved and elaborate Chippendale forms. 1. The example from the famous 'ribbon back' suite is directly comparable with the chair from Chippendale's *Director* (see page 28). 2, 3, 4. These are more or less influenced by a mixture of Rococo and French elements, adapted to the English taste, and are again expressive of the great variety of design and taste to be found in the middle of the 18th century.

5, 6. Such pieces as these, or provincial derivations, were to be found in most of the better English houses.
7, 8. Examples of simple rustic work in the style of the so-called 'Windsor' chairs.

31

1. The Chinese lacquered bed from Badminton compares with the Chippendale design opposite. Like the pie-crust table (4) it affords an example of the persistence of *chinoiserie* design, and above all, lacquer work, in the 18th century. The breakfast-table with its 'Chinese fret' follows directly a design from the *Director*, while the small tripod table (3) is typical of the period.

Further examples of 'Chippendale's' taste are provided by this second page of engravings reproduced from *The Gentleman's and Cabinet Maker's Director*, 1753 (see also page 28). Again variety is the keynote, and we find English and French, Gothic and Chinese idioms employed.

Adam

As in the case of Chippendale, Sheraton and Hepplewhite, the name of Robert Adam has become irrevocably associated with 18th-century English neo-classicism. In this case, perhaps, with rather more justification. Adam was the son of an architect, and collaborated with his brothers to become the leading architect-decorator of the 1770's. He spent some years touring and studying in Italy, acting as 'marchand-amateur' for antiquities and making drawings of monuments, and adapted these experiences to the decorative style already emerging from the Classical discoveries of previous decades, especially of Herculaneum and Pompeii. The result was the development still known by his name, and which was to influence not only England but the Continent as well.

As these engravings and his designs show, Adam liked to attend to even the minutest details.

The furniture here is either closely associated with Adam or actually designed by him. (2) and (5) show how closely the designs were often carried out. The very fine inlaid commode (6) is typical of the type of furniture which Adam used in his more elaborate interiors, and the candle stand (7) shows his imaginative interpretation of classical motifs.

5 6

7 8

9

8. In several houses Adam designed rooms in the French taste. The chairs must have been made for the Gobelins tapestry seats (*en suite* with the wall coverings, see page 43). The original Boucher designs are much earlier.
9. The cabinet was created for the Duchess of Manchester at Kimbolton to set off her collection of little Italian marble landscapes. Indeed, apart from two small cupboards in the sloping sides, the object serves no other purpose at all. The workmanship is of the highest order, and the motifs are typical of Adam.

We have already mentioned the tendency in English furniture design for a direct tradition of simplicity dependent on craftsmanship and respect for material persisting whatever vagaries of fashion might come and go. This trend is manifest in the design books, and in the pieces shown on this page, which date from the 1770's and 1780's.

1

2   3

While both the library table and chest (1 and 2) make some concessions to the new outlines, the source of their quality and merit is clear: the beautifully chosen wood and the balanced, elegant craftsmanship. The same applies to the table (3), though this and the rather more decorated commode owe some allegiance to the French influence.

4

Opposite page: The Glass Drawing Room from Northumberland House. Shortly after Adam's return from Italy the fabulously wealthy Duke of Northumberland employed him to remodel some of his houses. Two outstanding examples were Sion House near London, and Northumberland House, demolished in the 1870's to create what is now Trafalgar Square. It was from the latter that the famous Glass Drawing Room (1773-74) was taken. Presumably to represent red and green porphyry, the walls are sheeted with green and crimson glass set at the back with gold foil crumpled to create a glittering surface. Over this there is gilded classical ornament. The room must have made an impression of unbelievable luxury and richness when filled with people and lighted with candles.

36

This group of chairs shows trends active in the 1770's to 1780's. Some of these manifestly derive from the Chippendale period. The main difference from the mid-century lies, perhaps, in the framework which is much lighter.

1. This chair has still something of the traditional solidity, compared with the lighter (4). Both are otherwise closely similar and owe much to French taste.

2, 3. These also pay some tribute to earlier styles and French influence of the mid-century, but the oval backs make concession to the later fashion.

5. Of provincial origin, this shows a persistence of the Chippendale tradition in its square legs and splat back, though the corn husk motif and arched top rail of the back belong to a later period. Such pieces were much reproduced in the 19th and 20th centuries.

2

1

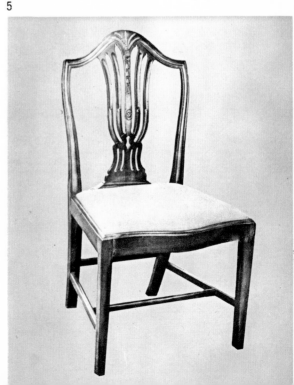

3

4

5

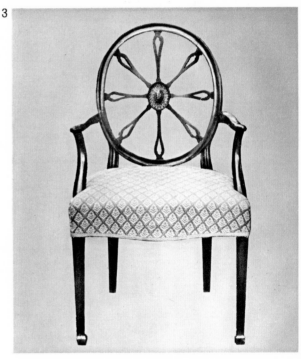

A more elaborate furniture style marks the last two decades of the 18th century. It coincides with the appearance of Hepplewhite's and Sheraton's books. As we know from the novels of the time, a new, wider public was concerned with display and status. Furniture is often rather affected in design, and there is particular emphasis on the demands of ladies.

To cater for this fashion, designs became more elaborate, and at the same time lighter both in line and in the use of lighter exotic wood, often with painted decoration. For such decorations, upholstery and backgrounds in light coloured silks, chintzes and embroideries were more popular than the heavier tapestry, leather and horsehair of the previous generation.

1

2

4

3

5   6

7

8   9

These features are clearly marked in the commode (1), the bookcase (2) and the chair (4), all of which give an impression of rather affected treatment. The legs of the bookcase and chair look almost too slight to bear any weight, whilst the elaboration of the painted decoration and flowers seems almost excessive, in combination with the already marked serpentine movement of the cabinet making.

At the same time, in their own proper setting these can look extremely attractive, and the craftsmanship is of the highest quality. Illustrations 5-9 are all characteristic examples.

The small chest (3) still retains something of the tradition of solid and 'sensible' design to which we have referred earlier.

1

2

The objects on this page, dating from the 1770's, reflect the classical influences as introduced by Adam and carried on by the next generation. Pieces such as this commode (1) appear frequently. The frieze motif, like that of the Kimbolton cabinet (page 35), is softened a little by the romantic feminine roundel and almost too-thin swags.

2, 3. Typical adaptation of neo-classical motifs.

4. The bureau-bookcase in satinwood leads on to the taste of the 1780's and 1790's. The overall design recalls Chippendale, but the lightness of the wood, floral swags and urns belong to a later period.

Opposite page: The superb Tapestry Room at Osterley Park House was executed to the last detail after designs by Robert Adam. Both the set of tapestries and the carpet were woven specially for the room.

3

4

George Hepplewhite

Almost nothing is known in detail of George Hepplewhite except that he was apprenticed in the north of England and then travelled to London. His *Cabinet Maker's and Upholsterer's Guide*, of which three editions appeared between 1788-94, does not aspire to great originality, but perhaps because of the popularity of Chippendale's *Director*, served to attach his name to furniture of the more exaggerated and affected type of the later 18th century. He drew readily from what had gone before and indeed does not pretend to great innovations. His declared aim, in the preface to the 1794 edition, was to 'unite elegance and utility'.

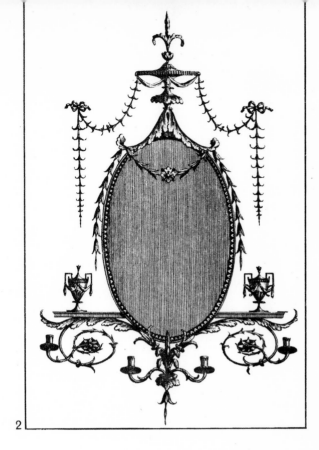

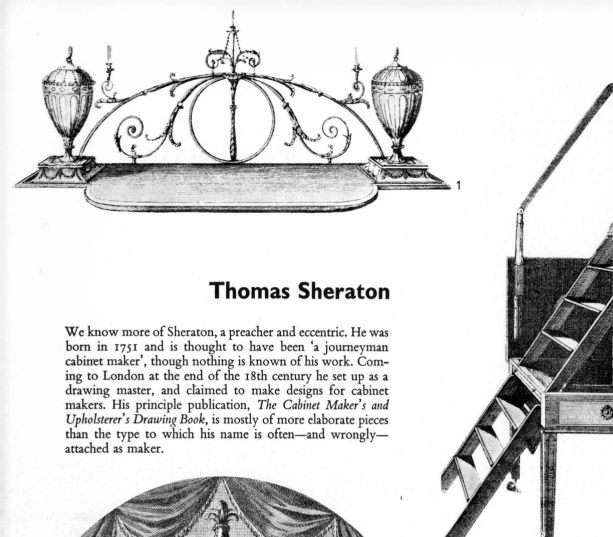

Thomas Sheraton

We know more of Sheraton, a preacher and eccentric. He was born in 1751 and is thought to have been 'a journeyman cabinet maker', though nothing is known of his work. Coming to London at the end of the 18th century he set up as a drawing master, and claimed to make designs for cabinet makers. His principle publication, *The Cabinet Maker's and Upholsterer's Drawing Book*, is mostly of more elaborate pieces than the type to which his name is often—and wrongly—attached as maker.

Nothing was lost of the very fine craftsmanship at the time of the Regency, which served as well for ordinary pieces as for the three very exceptional examples illustrated on this page.

1. The wall cabinet of inlaid mahogany is of the highest quality in its balance, elegance and fine cabinet making.

2. The same high quality of material and design is manifest in this seat made by March and Tatham for the Regent himself in 1802.

3. Another exceptional example of Regency in the simpler manner is this splendid library table designed by the antiquary Thomas Hope. The restrained classical ornament in relief sets off the superb timber. The whole depends on this emphasis of the best material and the best execution.

1   2

Regency

3

Examples of the more ordinary furniture of the period. 1. Shows the rather lugubrious solemnity of so many Regency rooms in the smaller houses of the time. 3. A very fine cabinet, still with much of late 18th-century design. 2, 4. The chair and table after a design by Thomas Hope represent a compromise between the more pedestrian objects and the extravagance of the later pieces.

1   2

3   4

Opposite page: This room is a modern reconstruction using Regency features, a decorator's reinterpretation of the 1800 idiom for the 1960's.

The mainstream of furniture design about 1800 reflects the severer neo-classicism general throughout Europe. Egyptian motifs were also to be found. The severity was in some degree offset by more elaborate upholstery and drapery than in the preceding period. Indeed the overall effect was often heavy, but must have been surprisingly colourful after the lightness of the later 18th-century interiors.

For once, considerable influence was exerted by the personal tastes of the sovereign—the Prince Regent, afterwards George IV. From his early days when Prince of Wales, the Prince had developed a passion for building and decorating houses. Unhappily his palace at Carlton House was destroyed, but much of the furniture has remained in the Royal possession. Within recent years his Pavilion at Brighton has been restored and serves to give us some idea of the succeeding fancies of this eccentric monarch. The earliest pieces are comparatively simple, but became increasingly fantastic as romantic-oriental elements became more popular with the 19th century.

1. An English rosewood commode of about 1820 with ideas derived from late 17th-century French Boulle.

2. A pair of white and gold doors from Brighton Pavilion, a combined Indian-Chinese fantasy, intended to go with the 'Indian' interests of the Prince. They date from between 1817 and 1823.

1

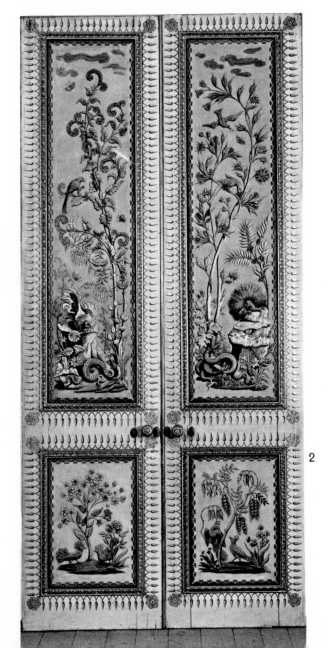

2   3

3. A chair, also from the Pavilion, shows how a lively imagination managed to combine a classically inspired framework with the Chinese taste currently attracting the Royal attention.

1. One of the most successful extravaganzas at the Brighton Pavilion is the Chinese Music Room in scarlet lacquer, with red and gold dragons supporting the ceiling, carvings, bells, fretwork and almost every decorative device. Something of this can be seen in this fantastic overdoor.

2. To accompany these oriental fantasies, furniture had also to be created, as witness this lacquer and bamboo commode. Something of additional fancy is added to such pieces by the fact that even the bamboo was carved out of solid wood and painted.

As the 19th century drew towards the third decade the division between the really extravagant designs for the rich and the more ordinary pieces became even more marked. Inspiration was sought from every source: romantic, medieval, Chinese, 18th-century French and Indian originals were all adapted to this decorator's extravaganza. Contemporary design books promulgated it and contemporary novels described it.

The Victorian room illustrated opposite shows the length to which this eclecticism and romance were to be carried in the mid-19th century.

THE LIVING TRADITION

Westwood Manor

This old stone house, dating from around 1500, was modernized about 1910. The original house was E-shaped with extensive wings, the centre block facing south. The wings have been in large part demolished, but their extent would account for the large scale of the remaining rooms.

1. A corner with an attractive turreted window.

2. The elaborate plasterwork of the chimneypiece, with its decoration of birds and beasts, foliage and siren motif, and the geometrical ornamentation of the ceiling are both typical features of the period. A Charles II armchair and Queen Anne wing chair stand either side of the fireplace.

All the rooms in the house have been thoughtfully arranged.

3. The tester bed and walls have been hung with Hungary stitch. 4. The table and stool stand in the embrasure of the window shown opposite (1). 5. The bed and coffer date from the 17th century. 6. A later bed of simple design with applied tapestry hangings.

3

4

5

6

The typical oak panelling reaches from floor to ceiling.
1. The 17th-century furniture includes leather-covered chairs of about 1650-60.
2. Old bottles and 18th-century tea caddies stand on an early dresser.
3. The window has leaded lights; on the early 18th-century desk is an ivory hourglass and clock of the period. The wall lights are of silver.

1

2

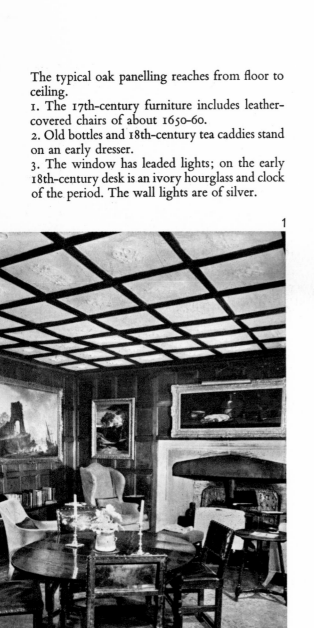

3

4

Foliage scrolls form a motif of the stucco ceiling.

4. A feature here is the door porch leading from the room with its fluted columns and carved frieze.

5. A general view showing furniture of the 17th and 18th centuries.

5

West Green House

1

2

1. This charming, simple house dates from the period of William and Mary. The large windows set in the red brick façade give great lightness to the interior, and are in strong contrast to the small openings of Tudor and Elizabethan houses. The niches with busts are a 17th-century feature, drawn from Continental sources, as are the small mansard windows which indicate Dutch influence.

2. The emphasis on simplicity is repeated in the interior with the simple line of the staircase. At the foot of the stairs is a William and Mary chest, on the landing a long-case clock.

3. and *opposite page:* Two views of the drawing room. The triangular pediments make an effective decoration to plain, simple panelling. A mixture of furniture, including Italian chairs, Hepplewhite seat and English tables, makes for an agreeable interior.

3

1

2

3

1. The furnishing of this dining room, with its plain folding table and provincial chairs, contributes to the studied simplicity of the decoration of the house.

2. The corner fireplace of this small study is original to the house. The Queen Anne chest of drawers is faced by a French fall front secretaire.

3. This hall was formerly the dining room. The niche houses china. In the 18th century such niches intended for display were sometimes made as separate pieces of furniture, sometimes built in, as in this case.

A remodelled farmhouse

2

3

Over the past half-century and more in England the conversion of Tudor farmhouses into modern homes has been very popular. Every effort is usually made to retain the outside appearance, while altering, or even gutting, the interior to make larger or smaller rooms as may be required. This example is typical.

2. A brick fireplace is set into the panelling. On the right an old farmhouse door with iron latch and wooden handle has been retained.

3. In the window is a collection of miniature furniture and silver. Such pieces were sometimes made by craftsmen as samples, or were made for dolls' houses.

Three views of the large living room. This gay, colourful room centres on the simple oak beamed fireplace, surrounded with deep sofas and chairs. The staircase and balcony lead to the first floor. Venetian lanterns hang from the beams and in one corner a bookcase and Regency table lend an air of intimacy.

1. Simplicity is again the keynote of this mid-18th-century manor house, with its plain grey stone façade relieved only by the mouldings round the windows and the pediment over the door.

2. The interior decoration dates almost entirely from the 19th century. Here a console influenced by the French Empire style and a Regency mirror stand at the foot of the staircase, which leads to a landing adapted as a small library (3).

The whole decoration pays tribute to French inspiration, and with the current French interest in English styles, affords an interesting example of the reciprocity of decorative taste.

1

Old manor house

2   3

1

2

1. The furnishing of this bedroom owes much to French late 18th-century, Empire and Régence designs. The combination is manifest in the bed, chair and stool.
2. The fireplace and mantelpiece figures show interest in the neo-classic.

Opposite page: 3. Here again the bed follows a Louis XVI design.
4. In this bedroom the treatment is rather restrained and more directly based on the Empire in style. The modern red wallpaper on one wall is decorated with Empire rosettes.
5. The plain dark-red wallpaper on the fireplace wall is chosen to emphasize the white of the mantelpiece. Two 19th-century footstools flank the fender.

3

4

5

1. An oval mirror of carved and gilded wood and Louis XV marble chimney-piece create a focus for this dining room. The taste for Continental forms is further shown in the chairs influenced by Louis XV design, the table itself and the swan-necked lyre-shaped firescreen.

2. and *opposite page*: The same heterogeneous assemblage—in this case of Empire, Regency and Victorian, with a fireplace of 18th-century design—and the variety of colours on the walls and upholstery is characteristic of a certain style of currently popular interior decoration.

Mompesson House

1, 2. This house near the Cathedral at Salisbury was first begun in the late 17th century. The façade facing the Cathedral is faced in stone; that at the back is of brick.

3. The hall has stucco decorations, in part of the period. The staircase has turned balusters; the *trompe l'œil* paintings are modern.

1

Two dining rooms have been created in the house. One is a smaller, intimate room (1 and 2) for everyday use, decorated in bright colours: red walls, blue carpet and flowered chintz curtains. The furniture is in the Regency taste.

2

3

3. The furniture of the more formal dining room is earlier. The variations in style are illustrated by the square legs of the sideboard in the large room, compared with the turned legs of the piece in the illustration above (1), and the inlaid panels in the one compared to the moulded treatment in the other. Otherwise the overall design remains basically the same. The deep side drawers are designed to hold bottles.

The main drawing room shows decorations in the style of the 1740's. This is particularly evident in the chimneybreast with its scrolls, foliage and broken pediment, and the mantelpiece with swag and masks. The Wedgwood vases, tables and chairs date from the latter half of the 18th century.
2. The stripped pine panel is a popular feature with English decorators. The woodwork dates from the first half of the 18th century; the fireplace is slightly later.
3. The white stucco decorations of the stair-well stand out against a Wedgwood blue ground.

71

King Henry's Hunting Lodge

1. An example of the English taste for follies, this small house in the Tudor style was built in the 18th century. The brick façade is flanked by a shepherd and shepherdess of the 18th century.

2. The main room on the first floor has been decorated with 19th-century needlework strips and small oval pictures of the same period. The painted chairs are 18th-century Italian.

3, 4. These two rooms again afford an example of the mixed taste in contemporary decoration.

ITALY

Introduction

From the dawn of history and long before it had any territorial unity, Italy has always been a centre where ideas and peoples from widely different horizons have combined to create some great artistic unity.

It was in this tradition that Florence, in the 15th century and under the aegis of the Medici, became the mainspring of that humanist awakening of the Renaissance which spread and influenced the whole of Europe.

At various times other centres played their part. The Venetian Republic, influenced by its wide maritime connections, developed its own styles, culminating perhaps in the luxurious villas along the Brenta.

Rome as the cradle of the Baroque, Genoa, Naples and the northern cities all played their part. Among these Turin, as the capital of the restored House of Savoy, was important to furniture design in the 18th century, particularly with its close adaptations of French models.

The discoveries at Herculaneum and Pompeii were all important in providing inspiration for the return to classicism in the 18th century, which was to reach its culminating point in Italy at the Napoleonic period. The tradition lasted long in the peninsula.

But above and beyond these individual stylistic contributions, the natural exuberance of the Italian spirit, which is to be found in every word and gesture of the daily life of the people, is reflected in the design and ornament of their homes.

AGNES MOUSNIE-LOMPRE

Frontispiece
The Annunciation by Carlo Crivelli

High Renaissance

The sumptuous decoration of Italian palaces set the tone for all European taste in the 16th century. A marked feature of the period is the elaboration of the ornament in which no surface is left untreated. As an example we have (1) the principle staircase of the Villa Cicogna with frescoed walls and ceiling. On another ceiling (2) the space between the beams is painted with armorial bearings.

1

2

3

Among traditional customs which persisted was that of the marriage coffer.

1. This example is said to have belonged to Ginevra Alighieri, a descendant of Dante's family, who married in 1549.

2. From another room in the same palace is a carved and gilded cradle, also traditionally associated with Ginevra Alighieri.

3. A fine Renaissance stone chimneypiece from the Bentivoglio Palace in Bologna.

1

2

3

From the Middle Ages in Italy walnut was almost exclusively used for furniture.
2, 3. Examples of a rustic type of three-legged chair well adapted for uneven earth or tile floors.
4. A Lombardy chair—interesting as an example of inlaid decoration of the small decorative panels.

78

4

5

6

1, 6. From the same region: These solid, heavy chairs might have rush or leather seats.

5. Folding chair. Such easily folded and transportable pieces were very popular at the Renaissance. They could readily be moved from one house to another.

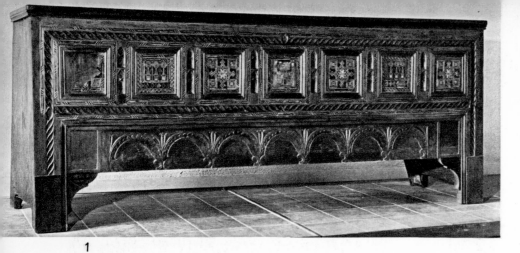

1

2

4

The coffer continued through the 16th century both as an object of decoration and serving a variety of uses: to keep things in, to put things on, to sit and even to sleep on. The design and ornament often varied considerably with the region. 1. An example from Lombardy. 2, 3. The classical elements appear early. Here we find developments of the classical garlands and carving in high relief of mythological subjects favoured in Tuscany. The angles often terminate in caryatids, and lion paw feet were popular. (3) is an elaborate Venetian example of a form adapted from the classical sarcophagus. 4. In the north, Gothic elements persisted later than in the south.

3

1

2

3

4

Late Renaissance

As the late Renaissance moves to Baroque,
decoration becomes ever more elaborate.

1, 2. Seat and armchair with elaborate, heavy
ornament of foliage, beasts and *putti*.

3. This provincial chair shows novel elements in
the carved back-rail and turned legs.

4. The usual scroll or foliage terminals are here
replaced by turned knobs. The leather on the seat
and back is attached by large decorative nails, a
practice maintained throughout the century.

The late 16th century saw an increase in heavy, stable, furniture often forming an essential part of the decorative whole.

1. Cupboards in two tiers became popular; this example in oak with moulded panels and spiral columns is almost northern in style. Tables with tops of marble or inset stones also enjoyed considerable popularity.

2. The influence of architectural design is manifest in this cabinet on a bracket.

3. It is also noticeable in this ebony cabinet inlaid with hard stones, ornamented with statuettes and appliques in gilt bronze.

4. A simpler example in light wood with moulded and inlaid decoration. Such pieces were often made to stand on a table. The doors open to reveal a number of small drawers.

1

2

Early 17th Century

1. Antechamber in the Castello di Colloredo
with stucco decorations. The windows have
wrought iron screens and elaborately painted
shutters. The chairs with turned legs and
leather covering date from the 17th century.
2. An old Bolognese kitchen retaining its
original equipment, copper and faïence pots
with an iron turnspit.
3. The entrance hall with leaded lights. The
two high-backed hall seats are of the 18th
century.

3

Four examples showing the development of the chest.

1. The bureau-bookcase with wide drawers below the writing section; above, the doors conceal further small drawers and shelves. This is a final development of the earlier portable writing chest mounted on another piece of furniture.

2. Cabinet on stand with decoration in ivory and ebony executed in the manner of Boulle work.

3. The coffer here has developed into a chest of drawers mounted on short legs.

2

1

4. Another cabinet with turned and moulded decoration on a stand with drawers. The central door opens to reveal perspective with geometric inlay. These decorative devices sometimes contain secret drawers.

3

4

Baroque

By the 17th century decoration in furniture follows the general exuberance manifest in all other arts. Carving and gilding are often pushed to extremes. 1. A marble-topped console table with *putti* and female busts among the foliage and scrolled supports. 2. Small tripod table with more restrained decoration in low relief. 3. Marble-topped corner console with almost Rococo frieze on a heavily-carved scroll support.

85

In the late 17th and 18th centuries the armchair becomes increasingly comfortable, with heavy padding or cushions upholstered in velvet or damask. The arms are generally shaped.

1. Here the back is 18th-century in outline, though the caryatids and apron are still in the 17th-century tradition.

2. The general shape and turning follow a simple 17th-century design common to Western Europe. The carvings at the joints and terminals of the arms are Italianate decorative elements of some originality.

3. Although the general form is still severe the ornament asserts its importance in the reclining nymphs, the little figures supporting the arms, the sloping back and carved apron.

Pure Baroque

In Italian Baroque furniture of the later 17th century the native Italian exuberance is sometimes tempered by the more measured classicizing influences which penetrated throughout Europe from Louis XIV's Versailles. The whole design becomes even more insistent, sumptuous and full, the ubiquitous gilding is in full accord with the Italian taste for luxury and display at that period.

1. A fine example with marble top resting on a tasteful agglomeration of *putti*, figures, foliage and drapery. 2. While still elaborately carved, this piece is less ebullient. 3. A Baroque development of the pedestal for busts or vases.

A group of elegant later pieces:
1. A small shaped cupboard with marble top in which the line of the legs follows into the carcase as part of the overall design.
2. A bureau-bookcase painted with the popular *chinoiserie* designs.
3. A semi-circular piece with lacework ornament recalling tooling stamps of the 18th century.

Opposite page: A painted Rococo bureau and display cabinet on which the delicate carvings are picked out in a second shade. To the left, a stand carved in the form of a Negro with polychrome decoration.

These illustrations show typical wall and ceiling treatments of the late Baroque. 1. An example of elaborate stucco work from the Palazzo Albrizzi at Venice. 2, 3. From the Villa Albergati. 2. The *Rape of Orynthia by Boreas* by Giovanni Antonio Burrini; the frame is painted in *trompe l'œil*. 3. An architectural perspective decoration by Angelo Michele Colonna.

4

5

6

4. Also from the Villa Albergati is this painted room by the Bolognese artists Pesci and Taliani. 5, 6. The exuberant ceiling of plaster drapery supported by flying *putti* is from the Palazzo Albrizzi.

1

2

We see here once again the play of French and Italian influences.
1. This settee bears strong affinities to early Louis XV design.
2, 3, 4. On the other hand these three armchairs demonstrate the
lengths to which Baroque exaggeration could be carried. The
interest here was manifestly as much—if not more—to create a
work of art in its own right, as to produce a comfortable and
practical chair.

3

4

Rococo

1. The chairs of this ballroom are gilded and upholstered in fine white and gold flowered silk. The graceful tables and mirrors too are carved and gilded. A chandelier and twelve wall brackets of crystal illuminate the room for formal receptions.

2. A view of a salon on the mezzanine floor of the Canossa palace at Verona. The walls of this room are decorated in the *chinoiserie* taste in shades of green, pink, yellow and grey. White and gold Venetian furniture, yellow and green floor tiling.

3. Anteroom in a Bologna palace: sofa and armchairs of the 18th century upholstered in Hungary stitch, and gilded Baroque table. On the wall, a large painting showing members of the Pallotta family (Ponte Brindisi, 1200).

93

1

In Italy as elsewhere the dining room was an 18th-century development; formerly trestle tables had been set up as needed. 1. A fine Venetian suite painted in tortoiseshell colour heightened with gold. The portraits of the Austrian Imperial family are set in carved and gilded limewood frames. 2. The decoration of the walls is afforded by the low stucco relief. The mahogany furniture suggests the influence of English design. 3. An alcove in which the Blessed Gregorio Barbarigo was born in 1655, transformed into a dining recess.

2

3

Opposite page: A charming example of elaborate painted and gilded decoration in an Italian room of the 18th century.

1. The chimneypiece of this small room, decorated with faïence tiles and *chinoiserie*, is surmounted by a two-tier mirror. The upper part is in three sections above a shelf. The door is surfaced with two mirrors in Rococo frames. Over the doorway, a cherub in a Rococo panel.

2. Another 18th-century example of a small faïence chimneypiece. Above, an 18th-century landscape painting by Vincenzo Martinelli and Pietro Fancelli.

3. Chimneypiece of coloured marble surmounted by an extremely fine mirror with carved frame, gilded and painted with flowers on a black ground. On either side of the fireplace stands a chair in natural wood heightened with gilding.

1

2

3

The mid-18th century saw a considerable expansion of the fashion for lacquered and painted furniture, as also of marquetry decoration.

1. A small, shaped commode with two drawers painted in white and gold.

2. Bureau commode (*ribalta*) in root walnut veneer with dark walnut moulded decoration.

3, 4. A bureau-bookcase and sideboard also veneered in walnut. The shaping is strongly marked.

1

2

3

4

5

6

5. An elegant and unusually wide console painted in dark colour and heightened in gold.
6. Small table with shaped tray top for bottles and glasses.
7. Painted and gilded console influenced by Louis XV design.
8. A typical 18th-century Venetian piece in ebony and gilded wood.

7

8

1

2

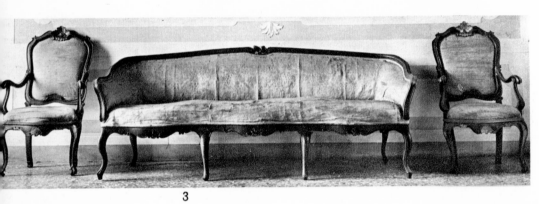

3

4

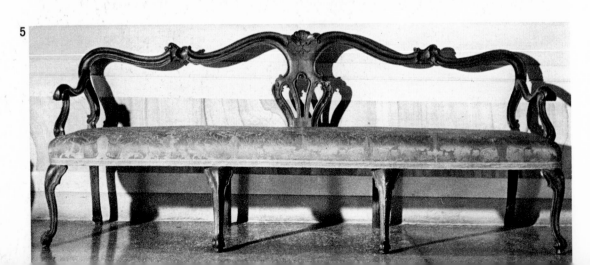

5

6

7

1, 2. The back of this seat swings forward to make a pew, for use in a private chapel.

3, 4, 5. Louis XVI influence is manifest in the first of these long seats. The open splats of (5) recall English design.

6, 7, 8, 9. All these four chairs suggest foreign influence. (6), possibly, and (8), manifestly, owe a debt to English examples, while (7) and (9) appear to be adapted from Louis XV and Régence originals. The wide leather-upholstered back of (6) and the similar feature in (7) betoken their Italian origin, as does the rather heavy treatment of the detail of the ornament on the other two. In such pieces the use of natural wood does not often occur.

8

9

1

2

4

Neo-Classicism

3

5

6

In Italy, as elsewhere, a reaction against the elaboration of earlier styles paved the way for a return to the Antique and a taste for simplicity.

1, 2, 3. Three views of the dining room from the Palazzo Dona at Venice.

1, 2. The Rococo console serves to accentuate the simplicity of the later chairs or the painted stucco panels in low relief with garlands, trophies and vases in the Louis XVI tradition.

3. The wall cupboard in the corner serves as a small oratory.

4. The Venetian gilt-metal bed with embroidered white hangings stands out against the turquoise silk covering of the walls.

5. Lord Byron's room on the first floor of the Palazzo Mocenigo. The original octagonal ceiling and wood marquetry of the alcove have been preserved. The door on the right leads to a private staircase.

6. An early 19th-century dining room with landscape wallpaper. The furniture bears eloquent witness both to French and English influences at the period.

1, 2. The simplicity and straight legs of the settees and chairs pay tribute to their Louis XVI origin, though the chair backs and padded upholstery mark a persistence of the richer Louis XV tradition ever popular in Italy.

3. The cane-seated chairs painted in white and gold again reflect Louis XVI influence, though the somewhat robust handling may be due to Austrian-trained craftsmen.

4. The northern Italian courts extended a ready patronage to the cabinet maker Maggiolini, to whom this cabinet is attributed. No less than twenty-six woods inlaid on a walnut ground give the effect of painting. Maggiolini's original designs were furnished by artists of the day.

Opposite page: A room from the Palazzo Giustiniani. On the walls are family portraits, giving a certain air of intimacy. The seats in light wood are decorated with pierced panels in black.

1

Early Empire

2   3

In the last years of the 18th and first of the 19th centuries the Napoleonic campaigns and the establishment of his puppets in various provinces of the Italian peninsula led to considerable exchange between France and Italy, and the establishment of a common style.

1. The furniture of this room and the severe treatment are an example.

2. The pieces here are largely Empire in conception, though retaining some features of the preceding period.

3. A bed in gilt metal recalling something of the campaign beds of the time. The hangings at the head and foot are of white satin embroidered with red wool.

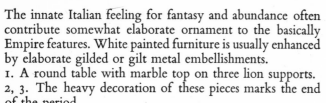

The innate Italian feeling for fantasy and abundance often contribute somewhat elaborate ornament to the basically Empire features. White painted furniture is usually enhanced by elaborate gilded or gilt metal embellishments.

1. A round table with marble top on three lion supports.
2, 3. The heavy decoration of these pieces marks the end of the period.
4. A somewhat finer decoration of fluted columns, garlands and classical heads serves to lighten this large chest of drawers.
7. The same principle applies to this settee as to (4).

5 6

The restoration of the Piemontese dynasty coincided with the Restoration in France, and in default of any immediate national tradition furniture styles in Italy follow those of Charles X and Louis-Philippe.
5. The fashion for natural wood in this chair and settee is typical of the mid-century taste.
6. Despite the carved lions and eagle, this dressing table in the bourgeois traditions of the day nevertheless remains rather undistinguished.

7

Carlo Felice

1

2

1. The individual pieces in this suite of polished mahogany dining room furniture are all designed to match. Though heavy they provide a solid and homely background.
2. The exaggerated height of this room presents some difficulties in furnishing; the large-scale overstuffed chairs emphasize the search for comfort.

THE LIVING TRADITION

Castello di Guarana

The present Castello was built about 1740 on the site of an earlier fortress, and the furniture and decorations fall between 1760 and 1770. It is situated on the summit of a Piemontese hill, surrounded by terraced gardens.

1. The structure is of brick with three tiers of windows. Those in the centre are in part blind, permitting rooms of great height on the ground floor without disrupting the balance of the façade.

2. A landing with painted *trompe l'œil* imitating stucco relief.

1. The main entrance hall dating from 1740 with a painted decoration of garlands terminating in mirror-shaped armorial shields. The arms are repeated on the benches. The floor is of marble, the doors are varnished wood.

2. The long gallery, lit by long windows on the east side, was decorated in 1770. The chairs and tables are French, the wallpaper and upholstery of the period.

Opposite page: The Chinese wallpaper in the small salon was acquired in London in 1774.

1

2 3

A contemporary Venetian apartment

The traditional Baroque decoration retains its period flavour.

1. A life-size stone figure stands at the bottom of the stairway; the handrail on the wallpaper is painted in *trompe l'œil*.

2. A painted Rococo commode stands beneath an elaborately-carved period mirror.

3. The 18th-century settee upholstered in red velvet is flanked by two white and gold consoles masking the radiator covers; above them, Rococo mirrors. The picture is set into a stucco moulding in the Venetian manner.

1

Comfort combined with elegance is the keynote of this large salon. The two sofas which stand on an Aubusson carpet on either side of the fireplace are of recent date, but in a traditional Piemontese style the upholstery is of faded red Genoa velvet. 2. A stucco niche follows the contours of the candelabrum and is lined with red to afford a contrast. Painted panels with scenes from the Commedia dell' arte have been set into the doors; the theme is carried on to the stucco reliefs over the doors (3).

2

4. A carved Baroque occasional table and 19th-century chair; in the background a painted Venetian Negro candle stand.

5. The dull gold velvet table-cover is held back by cords to show the stand, made out of a period Venetian torchère base.

6. A series of paintings has been set into a panel of stucco mouldings which follow the line of the sofa.

1

The entrance to this 16th-century palazzo is across the brick paved courtyard with stone inserts. 1. A wrought iron balcony. 2. An old Verona marble well.

Opposite page: Throughout the house the walls are of painted stucco, the floors of *terrazzo*. A Verona marble moulding surrounds the doors. One gilded and two painted armchairs surround the table with its cerise damask cloth. The gilt metal lantern, to which is attached a Venetian mask (*bautta*), is flanked by two oval north Italian paintings and four small glass pictures.

A palazzo at Verona

2

1. At the head of this finely-proportioned staircase a long-case clock of 1790 in blue, green and red stands against the rose-coloured walls. The steps, balustrade and figures are in pale local stone, the lamps of gilt metal.

2. A large mirror with gilt mouldings stands between the windows. The console is Venetian 18th century, the walnut and gilt clock bears the arms of Doge Falier. The figures are Capo di Monte.

3. The dining room has walnut furniture. The grey-white marbled walls have surrounds of pale yellow with almond-green moulded borders. The collection of Bassano and Venice wares with *chinoiserie* decoration in green, blue and yellow enhances the effect. A fine rare 17th-century Murano chandelier hangs from the ceiling.

1

2   3

A Paris apartment in the Italian taste

1. The elaborate Romantic doorway with mixed decoration of relief work and inlaid ivory designs, dating from the 19th century, sets the tone of this establishment.

2. In the entrance passage a gilded wood Venetian mirror finds its place among elaborate drapery and hangings.

3, 4. Italian elements such as the gilded Baroque console and tables, and the torch bearing figures have been married with Napoleon III chairs and a 19th-century Aubusson carpet.

5. Gold and silver add to the already exuberant effect of this dining room.

4

5

1

2

1, 3. Two *putti* heads support drapery hung behind the velvet upholstered bed. The mirror, chandelier and lights are of Venetian glass. 2. The centre panel of the elaborately carved altarpiece shows a *Descent from the Cross*.

3

1

A country house in the Friuli

1. The range of buildings was constructed in stages from the 17th to the 19th centuries. Nonetheless, the sections stand harmoniously among the trees and lawns.

2. The owner's study, where the decorations are those of a sportsman and collector. The modern weapons are arranged against a painted linen background. A group of old arms on the walls of the hall can be seen through the open door. The furniture is Biedermeyer, the stove of Austrian tiles.

2

1. The bed and chairs in this room are covered in glazed flowered chintz. The marble fireplace is set with Vietri tiles. A small show-cabinet on the commode houses a collection of Vienna porcelain. The Venetian glass chandelier is indebted to Dutch design.

2. The small ground-floor sitting room has upholstery in brightly coloured silk.

3

1

3. A traditional regional kitchen has been set up at the end of the dining room. Rustic chairs, copper pans and peasant pottery are ranged round the old open central fire. The dining chairs date from the 18th century.

2

Palladio

The classical villas built by Palladio or his followers along the Brenta and throughout the Veneto are among the most imaginative architectural developments of the period. Notable among these is the Villa Santa Sofia di Pedemonte on the Brenta near Verona. The original conception—of buildings surrounding an extensive courtyard, with a façade on a monumental scale—was never executed in full. All the rooms open on to galleries facing south towards the park, and the play of light on the ringed stone columns and balustrade set against the shade of the background serves to lighten a front that might otherwise appear somewhat squat.

1

3

2

1, 2. The vaulted ceiling and the pale-blue walls with white stucco panels ornamented with a light fret set off the marble floor. The Louis XVI white and gold furnishings are upholstered in heavy ivory silk with light-blue and yellow stripes. 3. The late 18th-century library chairs are of mahogany. The bookcase doors are painted in verdigris green picked out in gold against a darker green.

4. In the salon on the first floor is an elaborate mirror attributed to the carver Brustolon. The 18th-century furniture is upholstered in pastel silk.

5. The frescoed walls provide the main decoration of this ground-floor room. The painted candelabras rising from the dado give the impression of supporting a cornice hung with swags. The *Annunciation* to the right has at some time been partially destroyed by the insertion of a doorway. The sofas on either side of the chimneypiece are covered in white cotton with a pleated valance.

4

5

1

An 18th-century villa

2

3

3. Part of this gallery has been turned into a room furnished with fine Venetian chairs of the 18th century.
4. An 18th-century cut-board figure stands at the entrance of the door leading to the staircase.

4

1, 2. This villa offers a fine example of balanced proportion in the classical tradition. A long gallery cuts through the whole length of the main floor, opening to the south on to the entrance courtyard, and to the north on to the garden.

FRANCE

Frontispiece *La Grande Toilette*
Print after Moreau le Jeune

Introduction

Before turning to the study of French furniture it is not without interest to glance at the evolution of the French home, especially since this differs in some respects from that of the English speaking world.

In the manors or castles of the Middle Ages and even Gothic times the Great Hall was by far the most important feature, not only on the grounds of size, but also from its significance in daily life, since it was here that the family slept and ate, worked and entertained. Its decoration was virtually limited to wall hangings, either of costly fabrics or tapestries.

The 17th century witnessed a notable transformation as the fashion grew up of having a number of separate rooms designed for some specific purpose, such as ballrooms, gaming rooms, reception rooms and so on.

The same period saw the development of the 'private apartments', where the family might pass their private life in smaller and less formal rooms to which the word 'cabinet' was applied. In England, where smaller rooms were more general, this innovation had not the same significance, and the word 'cabinet' has indeed no immediate translation unless it is 'closet', though this scarcely embraces the range of boudoir, study, small library, or indeed any small room of the kind which came to be embraced by the word in France. These settings assumed an ever increasing significance, and by the 18th century, when French craftsmanship was at its height, the needs of these small rooms inspired many of their happiest creations. Settees and chairs had to be scaled down and special pieces such as dressing tables and small desks like the *bonheur du jour* were designed for women's apartments.

By the reign of Louis XIV, what we now term 'dining room' furniture evolved from the chairs, tables, sideboards and buffets designed for the special rooms which now began to be set aside for eating.

By the end of the 18th century the general lines of our contemporary house-planning had evolved. Whatever revolutions it may have brought for society, the 19th century introduced no significant developments in French furniture or homes, despite the luxury of the Empire and the pretensions of the Restauration. At the same time, in bourgeois homes the fashion grew up for decorating certain rooms in certain period styles, such as Renaissance or Empire for the study, Louis XV or Louis XVI for the living rooms, or Louis XVI for the salon. The tradition still persists, and helped by the distribution of reproduction keeps traditions alive in France.

JEAN DE HILLERIN

1

2

3

4

Late Gothic and Renaissance

Early furniture in France as elsewhere was simple and basic, limited to essentials such as benches, tables, coffers or chests.

1. The master chair, usually architectural in design, seems to have been the most elaborate piece in Gothic times. At the Renaissance it retained its significant proportions, but the style is Italianate.

2. An early example of the arm chair of a type known as 'caquetoir' from the early French word *caqueter*, to gossip. The tapering seat is supported on four turned column legs, the back rail is ornamented with architectural carving.

3. Half a century later, at the end of the 16th century, we find a slightly simplified version with cloth back and seat.

4. The 17th century saw the introduction of some ideas of comfort as in this chair with padded leather back and seat.

5. Coffer ornamented with finely carved caryatids and fantastic chimerae; the lion masks point to the period of Henri II.

Most Renaissance furniture is rather heavy, with elaborate carving and inlay of marble, tortoiseshell or metal, as in the case of this two-tier cupboard surmounted by a broken pediment (1).

Simpler pieces were not entirely excluded, as we can see in this elegant dresser (2) with ringed columns in the style of Jean Androuet du Cerceau.

3. The table was introduced to replace the board on trestles, and architects and craftsmen quickly developed elaborate designs, as in the case of this fine example with its arcaded central support.

4. Beds in the Middle Ages and Gothic times were sometimes slightly inclined; in the Renaissance they are horizontal, though the overall design with wooden head tester and corner posts remains, as in this example.

1

2

Louis XIII

The style generally termed Louis XIII begins towards the end of the 16th century and is marked by a fusion of late Renaissance and hispano-flemish elements.

1. Flemish tapestries on the wall and the painted ceiling with cupids and garlands of fruit and flowers introduce an air of luxury.

2. Louis XIII furniture like that of earlier periods is eminently suited to a country house, as shown by a Gothic chest and Louis XIII chairs against the plain walls and exposed oak stairs and beams.

3. The chimneypiece remains monumental in treatment and reaches from floor to ceiling. The masonry overmantel is often covered with panelling, sometimes elaborately carved or painted with fruit, flower or foliage ornament or strapwork cartouches.

Opposite page: This room in the Château de Brissac witnessed the negotiations for the reconciliation of Louis XIII with Marie de Medicis. The painted ceiling, tapestries and bed date from the 16th century, the chairs are Louis XIII.

3

Under Louis XIII the chair follows a logical development. The lightly padded seats and backs are upholstered in leather, Genoa velvet, flowered tapestry or Hungary stitch. The armed chair becomes a regular feature and the term armchair (*fauteuil*) enters into current usage.

1. This chair with spirally turned arms and stretchers and low back is characteristic of the time.

2, 3. Chair and armchair of about 1640. Towards the end of the reign the backs become higher, the upholstery more elaborate while scrolled arms and legs are introduced.

4. A heavy table, perhaps monastic in origin, is flanked by two benches with turned legs, upholstered in velvet.

5. Small stool with elaborately turned legs and a stretcher. A rectangular form with rounded edges was adopted for all formal pieces.

6. A provincial chair, table and cupboard. The silhouette remains substantially that of more elaborate pieces but the workmanship is cruder. The open back to the chair is a feature.

139

1. The panelled doors with cartouche decoration retain something of the Renaissance tradition.

2. This black wood table with shaped apron and 'X' shaped stretcher would have had an inset velvet or leather top. It dates from the end of the period.

3. High backed chairs with scroll feet, and a peasant table.

4. Heavy oak table with fielded panels to the drawers. The swelling and turned legs are reinforced by heavy stretchers. At the beginning of the 17th century writing tables were covered with cloths both on the top and hanging at the sides. The side panels were tied at the corners with ribbon. On use, the writer unknotted the front panel; the remaining sides served to protect the legs from draughts.

1

3

2

4   5

5. Richly-carved ebony cabinet in the Italian taste. The cabinet, set on a stand with turned legs, houses numerous small drawers ranged behind the doors. These served to keep papers, silver, jewellery and other such objects.

Louis XIV

1

These illustrations demonstrate the features of this period and mark the complete break with previous design. French furniture becomes increasingly independent of architectural forms and foreign influences. This applies as much to the heavy simple provincial examples as to the elaborate ormolu-mounted court pieces in fine woods.

1. A two-branch gilt bronze wall light. The plaque is decorated with a mask and acanthus foliage, which also appears on the hexagonal candle arms.

2. Fine chest by Charles André Boulle. The inlaid brass or pewter on a tortoiseshell ground is a feature of this maker. The handles, feet and escutcheons are of gilt bronze.

2

3

3. Against the painted panelling, carved with scrollwork, is a desk of the type known as 'Mazarin', a carved and gilded console table and a richly carved armchair.

1

2

3

1. A large display cabinet of ebony inlaid with brass.
2. Cupboard with marquetry of contrasting woods, a type of decoration probably developed from Holland.
3. The commode or chest of drawers is one of the innovations of this style and replaces the earlier coffer. Usually with three or four drawers with gilt bronze mounts. The earliest examples have matching wood tops which are replaced by marble in later examples.
4. Another example by Charles André Boulle, inlaid with brass. The low feet are typical, as are the shaped apron and the swelling front and sides.
5. The corner cupboard represents a further development of the commode.

4

5

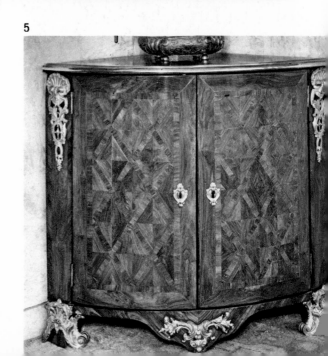

1

2

3

1. Boulle work is finely represented in this display cabinet and Mazarin desk. The general design of the latter is readily seen; the two ranges of drawers at the side are supported on legs held by shaped stretchers. The narrow recess with its cupboard in the centre is ill designed for comfort.

2. Fine clock with arched top resting on a tapering stand with short, peg-top feet. Such pieces herald the long-case clock.

3. Developing from the earlier writing table and the Mazarin desk comes another form of writing table—the 'bureau plat' —with a flat top resting on four legs, two pairs of side drawers and one central drawer.

4. An alternative shows three drawers set in the frieze. The decorated top is edged in gilt bronze, with mounts terminating in female busts (*espagnolettes*) and doe's-foot feet (*sabots pied de biche*).

5. Side-table of carved wood supported on eight baluster legs joined by an elaborately carved stretcher.

4   5

1. At the beginning of the reign, the search for comfort may take precedence over aesthetic considerations, as is witnessed by this wing chair designed to keep out draughts.

2, 3. Armchairs belonging to the opening of the period. One, in plain wood, is still in the Louis XIII tradition, the second in gilded wood is more elaborately carved.

4. Folding stool in gilded wood with tapestry cover.

1

2

3

4

5

5. By the early 18th century—at the end of the reign of Louis XIV—chairs become lighter, the stretchers disappear and the narrow backrail with higher central arching comes in.

6. Day-bed with richly carved legs and stretchers, upholstered in damask. The low headboard, like the chair backs, is entirely covered with material.

6

1

Régence

This period witnesses considerable changes of both form and decoration in furniture.

Two foreign influences play an important part: the Italian Baroque taste leading to Rococo mingles with the oriental. The contacts of the India companies brought a number of innovations to the decorative repertoire, with *chinoiserie* figures and landscapes, pagodas and exotic flora.

If the ornament is still elaborate, its treatment becomes lighter, mouldings are more refined, the outlines sharper. Chairs become a less important feature.

1. Here the panelling and cupboards are still Louis XIV in design, though the cane-seated chairs with 'X' stretchers are Régence. The table is a recent adaptation, the dining table as we know it had not yet developed at the period.

2. A silver wall light with an openwork backplate which is fully 18th century in design; the symmetry is typical of Régence taste.

3. A simple panelled room. A carved wood bed on which the shell decoration is more deeply cut than in the preceding generation.

2

3

1

2 3

Although still playing an important part in the general decorative whole, furniture becomes far less monumental in character and is adapted to the smaller and more intimate rooms, which were, incidentally, considerably warmer. Large pieces such as display cabinets (1) and wardrobes drop to a convenient height.

2. On this shelf silver candlesticks, ormolu clocks, vases and faïence from Nevers, Rouen, Marseilles and Moustiers, or porcelain from St Cloud could be set out.

3. The chimneypiece, whether of marble or wood, now takes the form of a surround to the fire, with a shelf above.

4. The commode retains three tiers of drawers but the shaping is more marked. Important pieces have rich marquetry.

5. A large alcove bed in carved wood. The knobs recall the plume terminals on Louis XIV testers.

4 5

1

2

Chair designs show a number of changes. There is considerable movement in the form; upholstery plays an all important part, the arms are in general open, and spring from the side frames; stretchers disappear almost entirely. The strip of back rail which is exposed is usually decorated at the top with a flower or foliage motif and scrolls at the end of the arms. Only the fronts are carved.

1. A long eight-legged settee stands below a Gobelin tapestry woven with a medallion of exotic landscape against a ground of flowers and trophies.

2. A fine carved and gilded armchair upholstered in floral tapestry, from the end of the period.

3. Carved and gilded wood stool upholstered in damask.

4, 5. The main difference between these two seats lies in the stretcher, denoting in the one case an early piece and in the other an example from the end of the period, moving towards the Louis XV style.

6. A small chair in natural wood; the form is designed to enable the sitter to straddle the seat and sit back to front.

3

4   5   6

1

Louis XV

2

1. This ormolu wall light emphasizes Louis XV asymmetry, line and decoration.

2. The Clock Room at Versailles with panelling of about 1760. The elaborate scrolls, volutes and garlands proliferate over both the panelling and the coving of the ceiling. The astronomical clock is housed in a Rococo ormolu case by Caffieri.

Opposite page: A group of Louis XV commodes. In general the carcase is raised on high legs and houses only two drawers. The top is always of marble (griotte, breccia, rance, campan, violette, rouge royal) which overhangs slightly and follows the contour of the furniture.

5. Corner cupboard with satinwood marquetry on a contrasting ground.

6. Large commode with a cupid's bow curved front. The absence of any apparent division between the drawers is another feature.

7. Medal cabinet of Louis XV executed in 1749 by Gaudreaux. Elaborate ormolu mounts almost obscure the marquetry.

8. Small commode with doors in kingwood marquetry, stamped 'Migeon'.

9. Small commode signed 'Boudin', with marquetry of three woods.

10. Far Eastern influences are manifest in this commode decorated with Chinese figures and motifs in gold lacquer on a black lacquer ground.

3

3. The natural oak panelling has been stripped. Originally the gilded relief and carvings would have stood out against a light painted ground. The chandelier is of ormolu with Meissen flowers. The commode with only two drawers has a marquetry decoration of flowers and musical instruments with ormolu mounts and handles.

4. A provincial room of the period.

4

5

6

7

8

9

10

Bureaux plats with marquetry decoration and ormolu mounts, sometimes with three drawers as in (2), or two pairs of drawers one on either side, as in (4), were popular for large rooms, but the ebenistes also designed new, smaller feminine models for more intimate rooms, such as the little *dos d'âne* desks, (1, 3). Sometimes these might have a fall front for writing, sometimes the high curved legs form a knee hole.

5. A small writing table with shaped top and fine floral marquetry.

6. Small kidney-shaped veneered table.

Opposite page: A fine typical oak panelled room of the period. The over-door is set into the panelling, the carving of the marble topped console blends into the woodwork.

1

3

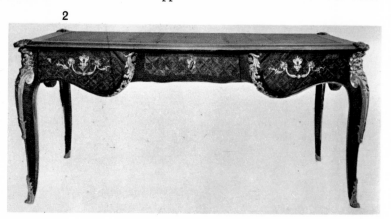

2

4

5

6

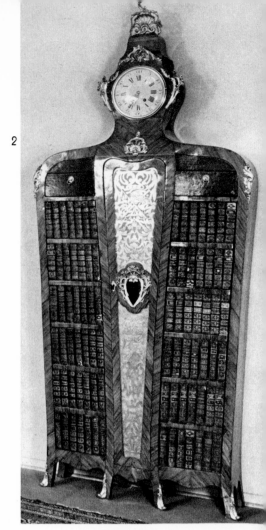

1. Wrought iron console table with gilded openwork cartouche and foliage decoration.
2. An unusual bookcase surmounted by a clock, and with small leather-covered drawers.
3. Another development of the period was the secretaire with a fall front for writing; above, a drawer, and below, a small cupboard with two doors.
4. Small cupboard with 'rouge royal' marble top and marquetry decoration in purple and kingwood.
5. Veneered lacquer cupboard with gilded decoration on a black ground. Ormolu mounts and moulding.

153

1. Small anteroom with painted panelling. The asymmetrical carving indicates the period. The elegant balustrade and stone floor with small black marble insets completes the atmosphere of elegance.

The five chairs illustrated on this page show the developments of this period.

2, 3, 4. These examples with their narrow arched backs and wide stretch of the arms belong to the first part of the reign.

5. This type, known as the 'cabriolet', was one of the most popular Louis XV innovations with its concave back, light carving on the top rail, at the knees and on the centre of the apron. The seats may be upholstered with a cushion as in this case, or overstuffed.

6. In this example, from the end of the period, the legs are still shaped but the back is simpler. The pearl-bead motif, so popular under Louis XVI, appears on the mouldings.

Opposite page: The element of comfort plays an ever increasing part and the padded enclosed armchair called a 'bergère' becomes, like the settee, an essential element in fashionable decoration.

7. A classic bergère stamped 'J. B. Meunier', in natural wood with a feather stuffed leather cushion.

8. A fine seat stamped 'Tillard'; the unusual design and rich decoration denote a cabinet maker of distinction.

9. A double seat known as a 'marquise', half bergère, half sofa, is another innovation of the period.

10. An elegant Louis XV ensemble.

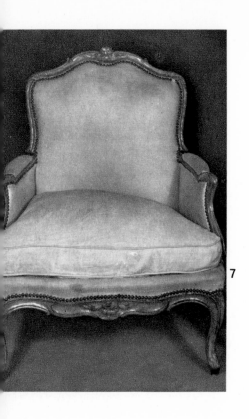

7

8

9

10

Louis XVI

Design under Louis XVI saw a complete change in forms of furniture, its decoration and even its material. The classical vogue, which had already swept England, played a considerable part in these changes in France. The first indications had been manifest in the previous reign.

1. One of Marie Antoinette's rooms in Versailles. The white and gold panelling with classical decoration, interlacing sphinxes, vases and so on, reflects the new taste. The square-backed chairs are signed 'Jacob'.

2. The panelling is divided by fluted pilasters with Ionic capitals.

3. Panelled library. On either side of the window are inset canvas panels painted with classical motifs.

1

2

3

1

3 2

4

1. The furnishing here tends rather towards the Directoire than Louis XVI, though the alcove is stretched with printed *toile de Jouy*.

2. Salon hung with tapestries of rustic scenes probably after designs by J. B. Huet. The medallion back chairs and basket shaped settee are from the same suite.

3. A corner of the King's Library at Versailles. Against the woodwork, with finely carved corner panels of garlands and trophies, stands the great bureau executed for the King by Oeben.

4. A Louis XVI dining room with white painted chairs upholstered in rawhide, a mahogany buffet with marble top and mahogany table. It is only at this period that special rooms set aside for dining and furnished for the purpose make their appearance. Hitherto, trestle tables had been brought in for meals and removed afterwards.

3

1

5

2

4

Opposite page: 1. A fine transitional commode. The marquetry and mounts are in the full Louis XVI taste though the shaped feet recall the preceding reign.
2. Another commode with flower marquetry.
3. A third transitional piece of a design known as *à la Reine*. A number of examples of this period show the fronts divided into three upright sections with the centre portion brought slightly forward.
4. The feature is marked on this example with diamond pattern marquetry.
5. Classic commode in marquetry termed *à la Capucine*. The name was applied to pieces in plain wood.

This page: 1. Another view of the King's Library at Versailles. Typical features of this type of commode are the angled pilaster corners and peg-top feet.
2. A richly-mounted commode is flanked by oval backed chairs. The ribbon bow motif at the top of the backs was a popular decorative element at the time. The arms, while sweeping back slightly, rest directly on the front legs.

1

2

159

The Louis XVI chairs illustrate the different forms of seat which were adopted at the time.

1. Square backs and slightly tapering seats were popular with the great maker Jacob.

2. Caned chair with lightly arched back and squab cushion seat.

3. The curved back rail terminates in two small squares decorated with rosettes. The edges of the seat are rounded.

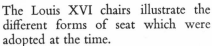

4. The oval medallion backs are sometimes almost round; the seat is nearly circular.

5. Lyre back chair; such openwork decoration was popular under Louis XVI. The tapering of the back is repeated in the seat.

All these examples show straight turned fluted legs; in (4) the fluting is spiral.

6. An alcove in Mme Dubarry's library at Versailles. Against the Louis XV panelling are chairs in the Louis XVI style, which had indeed begun at the time of this last favourite of the King.

Opposite page: Dining room with decoration and furniture in the Louis XVI tradition. Painted wallpapers were introduced at this period. Royal patronage was accorded the Manufactory of Reveillon on 13th January, 1784.

All chairs at this period were painted, apart from the most important which were gilded.

1. Small chair like a Louis XV cabriolet.
2. Large bergère with small feather-like terminals.
3. Directoire characteristics are to be found towards the end of the Louis XVI period. Here the severe form is manifest in the square back and turned arm supports rising directly from the front legs.
4. Settee with eight legs painted in light 'Trianon' grey.
5. A marquise or large bergère designed to seat two.
6. A Louis XVI salon. The chairs have medallion shaped backs and squab seats. Painted in two tones of Trianon grey bordered by a fillet of green, blue or red.

The fall front secretary or desk (*secretaire à abattant*), introduced under Louis XV, continued in full fashion. Marquetry of light woods still remained popular but mahogany was also used. The marble tops were often bordered by a light gilt bronze nail.

1. A large example in figured mahogany relieved by gilt metal border strips; the top is of marble.

2. Another example in marquetry.

3. Another in marquetry diaper.

4. A chiffonier, sometimes called a 'semainier' from the seven drawers, one for each day of the week.

5. A fine secretaire with *chinoiserie* decorations, stamped 'Roentgen'.

6. An Amboyna cabinet on stand executed by Weisweiller for Marie Antoinette. A panel of soft paste Sèvres porcelain is set into the front. The square tapered legs held by an elaborate openwork stretcher was a popular style for the small cabinets, desks and writing tables designed for ladies.

7. Salon furnished with fine pieces of the period; a pair of bergères, an occasional table, a worktable and, by the fireplace, a large mahogany filing cabinet.

1

2

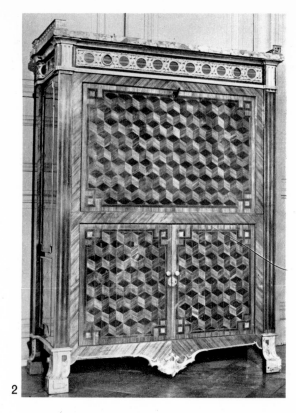

3

4

5

6

7

Directoire

The influence of the Antique becomes increasingly marked under the Directoire.

1. Small chair with open scrolled back and a severe mahogany desk.

2. Bergère. The Louis XVI design shows modifications in that the detached arms and plain turned legs are no longer fluted, though the rosettes still feature at the joint.

3. Mahogany now comes into more general use, as in this leather-covered chair.

4. Small armchair upholstered in striped silk which was popular at the time.

5. Another armchair. Formal classical decoration.

2 3

Opposite page: A number of Directoire elements feature in the decoration of this dining room: the marbled niche; the scroll back chairs; the table with legs adapted from animal forms—an Etruscan contribution; the rectangular mouldings of the pine panelling painted in two tones and the small wall lamp which marks the beginning of oil lighting.

4 5

1. The stone floor of this circular antechamber is decorated with black marble insets. The wide fluted Doric columns recall Greco-Roman temples. The marble top of the small centre table is supported on bronze legs with gilt enrichments. The seats derive from Roman designs.

1   2

2. The small Directoire bed is painted in two tones, the pediment and pineapple knobs at the head and foot are characteristic.

3. The fine day-bed and scroll back chairs are a feature of this room.

3

Empire

Under the Empire the fashion for using mahogany with gilt bronze enrichments dominates all furniture design. A few exceptions occur, such as painted chairs in white and gold. The designs of the popular ormolu mounts are always adapted from classical sources and include palmettes, acanthus, winged sphinxes, dolphins, swans, heroic heads and so on. Classical figures were popular, occasionally combined into the Imperial emblems of the bee, the eagle and stars.

1. Gilt bronze wall light showing a winged figure supporting a ring, with spread eagles bearing the sconces.

2. A mahogany library; the cupboard doors have bronze appliques showing female heads within laurel wreaths and rosettes. The pilasters dividing the shelves have metal capitals.

3. A mahogany table with column legs terminating in metal sphinx heads; palmette appliques are used to decorate the frieze.

4. Two mahogany scroll-back bergères of Directoire design stand one on either side of the mantelpiece, the shelf of which is supported on sphinx heads resting on animal legs.

5. Occasional table (*guéridon*) in bronze with gilt bronze enrichments; the legs are again sphinxes resting on animal legs.

6. Mahogany bed; the semi-circular treatment of the front led to the term '*lit bateau*'. Secretaire with detached columns.

7. Oval room decorated with a scenic wallpaper, '*Paysages d'Amérique*', by Zuber. The bed shows a characteristic feature in which the column against the wall is higher than that in front.

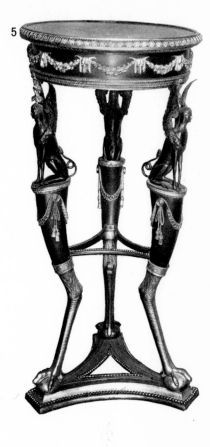

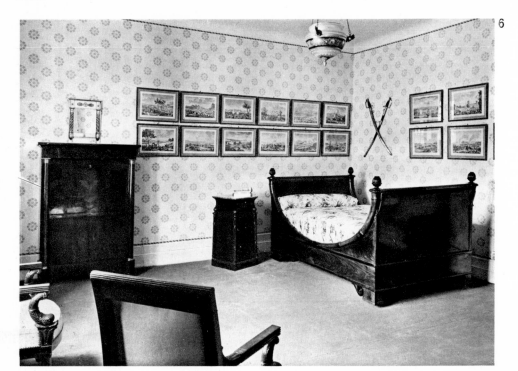

1

2   3

4

1. On this small mahogany cupboard the decoration is restricted to the plain pilasters with metal caps. The chair rail terminates in small ram's head masks.
2. Mahogany chair with dolphin arm supports.
3. A new form of day-bed called a 'méridienne' replaces the traditional form. There is no foot, and only a low short back terminating in a carved swan.
4. A typical Empire mahogany group of secretary, armchair and stool.

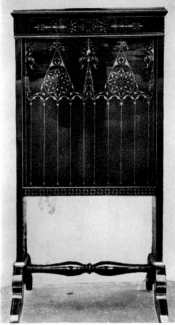

Restauration

The Restauration brought in few marked changes in basic design. The Empire line is, in general, somewhat softened, and the use of gilt bronze less lavish. This sometimes tends to make the pieces somewhat sombre. A rather wider range of woods is employed, including figured mahogany, satinwood, burr ash, elm.

The period is marked by three phases. During the reign of Louis XVIII a bastard Empire style continues, with mahogany still the principle material. Under Charles X the taste for light woods and inlay prevails; at the end there is a short romantic period and the appearance of neo-gothic.

1. A Charles X dining room in satinwood and burr elm. The barometer on the wall set in a *verre églomisé* frame marks a new departure.
2. Folding writing desk with neo-gothic inlay in satinwood.
3. A lady's dressing table on which square scrolled legs with paw feet have replaced the Empire animal legs or columns.
4. Side-table in figured mahogany.

1

1. Small Charles X salon with typical bureau, occasional table and scroll armchairs in light wood, and a severely designed filing cabinet with leather-covered drawers.

2. Two méridiennes with low ends flank the fireplace. Here they are used standing freely in the room rather than against the wall.

3. Charles X dining room. The form of scrolled arm was popular at the time.

4. Louis XVIII secretary and small chair with open-work splat back of palmette design.

5, 6. Two Charles X pieces in light wood with metal handles.

7. Satinwood bucket chair with palisander inlay.

8. Méridienne in mahogany with light wood inlay.

2   3

4 5

6

7

8

Louis-Philippe

This reign gave little encouragement to imaginative creation. A spirit of economy reigned and influenced fashion. The result was a bourgeois style of little originality.

In decoration, wallpapers, elaborate draperies and glass domes set the order. Innovations included the wardrobe with mirror doors, an armchair known as the 'Voltaire', and the piano stool.

Ormolu mounts and inlaid decoration declined, and as a result the pieces take on a heavy air. Such relief as existed depended on the inherent quality of the woods used—figured mahogany, palisander and so on.

Small pieces and chairs, generally based on Louis XV designs, were mounted on castors.
1. Mahogany occasional table flanked by two cherry-wood chairs.
2. Salon furniture derived from the preceding period. The table has a grey marble top.
3. Small desk with turned legs.
4. A comfortable sofa; the design recalls the effect of two méridiennes placed end to end.

5   6

8   7

5. Small mahogany secretaire of a popular type; the front falls to reveal small drawers in light wood. The only ornament is provided by the small circular handles and lock plates.

6. Mahogany chair and a wardrobe veneered in light wood with moiré-like veining.

7. Writing desk which is basically a chest of drawers surmounted by a writing element.

8. A veneered dressing table; the exaggerated shape of the legs is a feature of the period.

177

Napoleon III

This period sought to borrow from every preceding style, often mixing several different elements in the same piece. The result makes for confusion and over-elaboration. Two innovations were the chair upholstered in buttoned material, and the use of papier mâché.

1. Small chair upholstered in buttoned material and hung with elaborate fringed drapery.
2. Sideboard in black wood with painted borders and flower sprays.
3. A room of the period. The chairs are of dark wood with buttoned decoration. The table has a shaped top developed from Louis XV.
4. Ebony veneered desk with elaborate brass and shell inlay in the Boulle tradition.
5. Méridienne overstuffed with buttoned material, the framework bound and edged with braid. Only the wood of the feet is exposed.

6

7

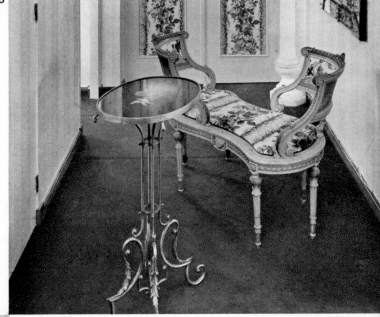

8

9

6. Salon decoration based on Louis XVI designs. The black wood is heightened with gilding. The table is covered with heavily fringed drapery. Fringes and heavily embroidered trimming were widely used during the period on curtains, hangings, valances and so on.

7. Gas bracket in bronze with gilt decoration.

8. A 'confidant', a small double seat designed so that the sitters could face each other. Other versions might be in a spiral form to seat three people. Again, buttoned upholstery was frequently used.

9. Table in a pastiche of Venetian 18th century, with a gondola-shaped chair of papier mâché decorated with elaborate lacework and coloured flower sprays on a black ground.

179

1

2

In the Ile St Louis

An apartment in the heart of Paris, the Ile St Louis, decorated by André Deveche.

1. The opening of this doorway between the salon and anteroom is outlined in the 17th-century taste with a carved and gilded moulding.

2,3. Two views of the salon. A traditional open beam ceiling, and parquetry floor. The walls are hung in lime silk set off with panels of Hungary stitch.

Opposite page: Another view of the same room with Régence chairs, a sofa upholstered in a red damask to match that at the back of the recess. The woodwork is white with gilded moulding and carvings.

The walls of the lower room are stretched with an unglazed chintz of Chinese motifs on a white ground, with applied border and medallions of the same material in red and blue.

3

1. The walls are stretched in moss green velvet. A fine gilded wood console stands under a panel of mirror.
2. The hall is lighted by an old window in the salon wall.
3. A panel of *petit-point* framed in gilded wood has been set over the door in the 18th-century manner.
4. The radiator cover is of framed material panels.

1

2

3

4

1 2

Château in the lle de France

3

Nothing remains of the original 16th-century building except the foundations and moat. The two present blocks of buildings facing each other date from the 18th century.

1. The pavilion in the photograph is arranged as a museum of furniture.

2. In the hall, family portraits have been let into the panelling. The medallion over the mirror is of Mlle de Blois, daughter of Louis XV. The chairs are Régence; the sedan chair on wheels belongs to the late 18th century.

3. Corner of the small salon. The boiseries are Louis XV, the chairs Louis XVI.

Opposite page: 4. In front of the painted 18th-century screen are transitional Régence-Louis XV chairs and a Louis XV commode.

5. A fine series of volumes from the Library of Colbert are housed in glazed mahogany bookshelves. The settee, chairs, stool and table are early Restauration.

4

5

The Château de Buzay

2 1

3

1. The south front opens into the courtyard. So harmonious an arrangement with its columned portico and a pediment inevitably suggests the architect Jacques-Ange Gabriel. The decoration and furnishings have remained virtually intact since they were installed by the original owner.
2. The portrait above the chest of drawers in this small salon is by Largillière.
3. The Indian print counterpanes, covers and curtains have been in place for at least one hundred and fifty years.

Opposite page: The main salon painted in white and gold with gilded Louis XV and Louis XVI chairs. In the foreground is a Louis XV dressing table.

4

5

The Château de Buzay

2

1

3

1. The south front opens into the courtyard. So harmonious an arrangement with its columned portico and a pediment inevitably suggests the architect Jacques-Ange Gabriel. The decoration and furnishings have remained virtually intact since they were installed by the original owner.

2. The portrait above the chest of drawers in this small salon is by Largillière.

3. The Indian print counterpanes, covers and curtains have been in place for at least one hundred and fifty years.

Opposite page: The main salon painted in white and gold with gilded Louis XV and Louis XVI chairs. In the foreground is a Louis XV dressing table.

Some private houses in La Rochelle

The notable houses in La Rochelle bear witness to the prosperity of the port in the 18th century. The ship-owners and merchants of the day created some magnificent interiors, which remain unchanged to this day.

1. Hall of the Hôtel Poupet—now the Préfecture—with its original Louis XVI frieze, pediment, fluted Doric columns.

2. Louis XVI chimneypiece and panelling in the main room of the same house. In contrast to those of the previous period the overdoors are in relief.

3. Another house in La Rochelle. Flemish tapestry on the walls, Régence tapestry chairs, and a commode with elaborate mounts, on which are two cut-glass girandoles.

A Country House

1

2

3 4

Provincial pieces or Restauration furniture are best suited to country-house decoration.

1. The façade has been covered with trellis work for climbing plants and roses by the artist-owner, M. Chapelain-Midi.

2. Simple wood benches and rush seat chairs are placed round the long table. The door mouldings of the provincial Louis XV buffets match the panelling.

3. A large comfortable sofa upholstered in Genoa velvet faces the fireplace. The small Directoire white faïence stove serves as a table; the chairs are Louis XV.

4. Guest room with chintz paper walls; the chair is Napoleon III, the light wood desk is inlaid with palisander.

5. The ceiling beams are painted in blue and white against a yellow ground. The mahogany bed, dressing table, and other furnishings are all Louis-Philippe.

5

1

2

The Château de Chambonas

1. View through the chestnuts across the plain of Vans. The 15th-century fortified house stands on a fine terrace.

2. The painted *chinoiserie* flower decoration of the vaulted ceiling recalls that of the Bishop's Palace at Viviers, executed after 1732. At various times Chambonas has had family connections with the bishops of the Vivarais.

3. In the salon, the vaulted ceilings are still a feature; the stucco decorations date from the 18th century. The fine Régence and Louis XV furniture is set off by the Savonnerie carpet and white painted tile floor.

3

HOLLAND

Frontispiece
Family Group by Adriaen van Ostade

Introduction

Henri Asselin once wrote of the Dutch that the house, or perhaps rather the home, in Holland was 'toute une institution' and that in his attachment to it the Dutchman 's'extériorise dans son intérieur'.

As early as the beginning of the 15th century the brothers Van Eyck painted such an interior in all its intimate detail—a detail that could only have been created among a people deeply conscious of the significance of the home.

Two centuries later we find a similar reflection in the early pictures of Pieter de Hooch, Jan Steen or Emanuel de Witte, whose interior scenes are presented as an integral, indispensable part of life. Similarly the interiors of Jan Vermeer offer an inimitable expression of the bond between the people and the surroundings in which they lived.

It is at this period that Dutch furniture assumes its most characteristic forms. The monumental cupboards, massive tables and chairs with their stout baluster legs all serve to epitomise the spirit of a people ever ready to champion freedom, and to combat any threat to its independence.

TH. H. LUNSINGH SCHEURLEER

Gothic

1

2

3

4

5

At the end of the Middle Ages furnishings were still sparse in the Low Countries. Oak was the principal material.

The master chair (2) was the main feature of the room. Linenfold panels formed the usual decoration, as in the case of the bench with movable back (5) which would normally have stood before the fire. Such pieces also served as coffers. The Renaissance saw the introduction of the light armchair with slender columns forming the arms and legs (1, 4). These were similar to the so-called *caquetoir* in France.

6   7

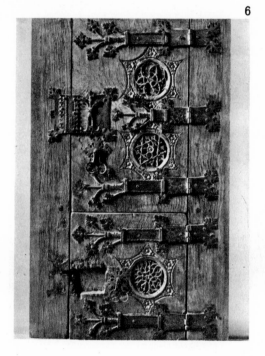

8

Wing chairs designed to keep out the draughts were ranged on either side of the fire and reserved for special guests. (3) was used by William of Orange on a visit to the Burgomaster of Amsterdam in 1578.

Small cupboards (6) were often decorated with elaborate ironwork sometimes sheathed with pewter. The large cupboards with drawers (7) were only used by churches. The coffer (8) shows decoration adapted from classical sources.

Early Renaissance

1. Cupboard in two tiers decorated with Gothic tracery and pinnacles. 2. Early 16th-century dresser. An unusual piece from the Arquebusiers Company of Alkmaar, carved on all four sides. 3. Court cupboard with caryatids representing Faith. 4. Draw-end table in walnut with chimerae and arches characteristic of the designs of Androuet du Cerceau.

3 4

High Renaissance

Robust construction and good proportions are a feature of Dutch chairs of the first half of the 17th century.

1. An 'X' chair in walnut with reliefs of marine monsters, half human and half dolphin. These often appear in paintings of the time. Palisander wood was used for the finest examples (2, 3, 5, 6).

2. The arcading is typical of this type of seat.

3. A magistrate's chair with openwork decoration.

4. A similar example in walnut.

5. The spiral turned leg became general in later examples.

6. Chairs with such slender column legs appear round about the 1640's.

1. A small cabinet on table base, its doors decorated with allegorical figures; to the left, a walnut folding chair for use in church. 2. A desk dated 1628 showing close affinities with the Spanish bargueño. 3. Bench in the form of a low table. 4. Table veneered with palisander wood and ebony. 5. Oak table designed to be folded against the wall when not in use.

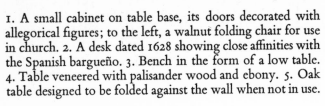

6

7

In the 17th century the cupboard becomes the most important piece of furniture in the room. The designs often enable us to assign a regional provenance. 6. The caryatid supports represent Faith, Hope and Charity; the reliefs illustrate the story of Susanna. From southern Holland. 7. Cupboard with wide doors decorated with ebony panels, originating probably from Guelderland. 8. Elaborate cabinet veneered in ebony and ivory, possibly from an Antwerp workshop. 9. A typical example from Zeeland.

8

9

1

2

3

4

1. Oak bed incorporated in the panelling, from Zeeland.
2. Bed of palisander wood with decoration in marquetry and
ivory inlay which must have been made for a person of distinction. The curtains are of pearl-grey flowered damask. 3. Chimney-piece of the early 17th century, the shelf resting on stone
columns. Above, a painting by Jan van Bijlert. The walls are
stretched with Hungary point. 4. Another bed in the panelling,
from Utrecht. The walls are covered with Hungary point.

Baroque

After the Revocation of the Edict of Nantes (1685), the Louis XIV style appears in Holland. Among the refugee artists Daniel Marot exercised a profound influence on the interpretation of this style, notably in the State beds which came in about 1700.

1. The woodcarving is a salient feature of this bed. The head and footboards are covered in damask ornamented with a fringe (from the Castle of Amerongen).

2. Bed with pale green damask curtains from the Castle of Eerde.

3. Bed with curtains of multi-coloured cut velvet, about 1690, from the Castle of Rosendael. According to tradition it was kept for visits of Queen Mary of England, wife of William III.

1

2

3

1

2

From about 1640 the chimneypiece derives from classical architecture. 1. Example in wood painted green and gilded, from a house in The Hague. The painting is by Th. v.d. Schuer. The walls are stretched with gilded leather (*c.* 1700). 2. Chimneypiece of carved wood designed by the architect Philips Vingboons in 1639, from a house in Amsterdam. 3. Frame of carved and gilded wood; about 1660.

3

5

6

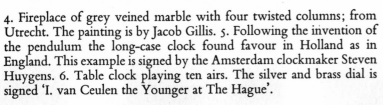

4. Fireplace of grey veined marble with four twisted columns; from Utrecht. The painting is by Jacob Gillis. 5. Following the invention of the pendulum the long-case clock found favour in Holland as in England. This example is signed by the Amsterdam clockmaker Steven Huygens. 6. Table clock playing ten airs. The silver and brass dial is signed 'I. van Ceulen the Younger at The Hague'.

1

2

3

4

5

6

7

8

1, 5. Rather disproportionately high-backed chairs typical of the style of William II of Orange. 2. Folding seat, for use in church, in palisander wood (c. 1650). The spiral twisted stretchers recall an early style. 3. Tapestry covered stool. The carved stretcher is of French origin. 4. Rush seated chair. Its origin is frankly peasant, but the design and quality class it with the burgher furniture of the day. 6, 8, 10. Caned chairs showing the development of this type which enjoyed great popularity from about 1670 into the 18th century. 7. Armchair in walnut (which began to replace oak from the mid-century), covered in red and green velvet; late 17th century. 9. Wall seat in walnut with carved back of Baroque design. Such pieces can be regarded as particularly Dutch, though deriving perhaps from Spain. Rather similar ornament is to be found in Italy at the period.

9

10

1. Cabinet with two doors decorated with floral marquetry attributed to The Hague craftsman Philips van Santwijck. This piece, which dates from about 1680, is in marked contrast to the imposing example (2), dating some twenty years earlier and veneered in ebony and decorated with twisted columns, fielded panels and heavy cornice.
3. Double cabinet. The floral marquetry signed with the letters F.V.G. and the word 'Grabant'.
4. Cabinet veneered in palisander and ebony.
5. Cabinet decorated with engraved mirrors; the doors veneered in acacia wood.

6

7

8

9

6. Walnut table with baluster legs; dating about 1700.

7. Carved and gilded table of the early 18th century. The caryatid legs represent the four seasons.

8, 9. Such late 17th-century tables with floral marquetry were designed to go against the wall. They were sometimes accompanied by two candle stands and a mirror *en suite*.

1

2

1. Reconstruction of the interior of a rich burgher's house of the 17th century, in the Museum at Utrecht. The floor is of black and white marble slabs; note the baluster legged table. Over the veneered walnut cupboard is J. G. Bronckhorst's *Musicians*.

2. Reconstruction of the corner of an Amsterdam room with a group of typical burgher's pieces of the 17th century.

3. To the left a door-frame in oak and palisander from Zeeland (about 1620), and a fine cabinet with star pattern inlay of the late 17th century.

Opposite page: This kitchen with walls covered in Delft tiles houses an interesting collection of faïence plates. The country rush seat chairs are of a regular type.

3

1. Saloon of the Castle of Amerongen erected after 1672. At either end are chimneypieces supported on marble columns; against the walls family portraits and a cabinet of floral marquetry. The carved and gilded wood furniture is stamped 'Lelarge'; the bergères are by The Hague cabinet maker Adam Struys.

2. Stucco ceiling with a grisaille painting of *Aurora* by Willem van Nymegen.

3. Stucco ceiling of the grand double staircase of the Castle of Middachten.

1

2

Dolls' houses

The name 'dolls' houses' may perhaps give rise to a misconception that these pieces were designed for children, which was not in fact the case. In the 17th century the rich burghers of Amsterdam employed a great number of artists and craftsmen, painters, sculptors, cabinet makers and goldsmiths to create interiors of considerable refinement. These models were designed to transmit an image of the surroundings in which they lived to their descendants.

The example (2) above shows every room in the house reproduced down to the smallest detail. The artists themselves made these miniatures. Such dolls' houses usually descended in the female line.

1. Dolls' house of Petronella Oortmans (*née* de la Courte), made in Amsterdam in 1680. 2. Ground floor: to the left a kitchen and bedroom. 3. On the first floor: to the left a drawing room, right a collector's study.

3

4. An example housed in a cabinet of tortoiseshell and pewter, made towards the end of the 17th century.

Here we have a kitchen with painted *trompe l'œil* ceiling. 5. In the bedroom, the walnut bed is recessed in the alcove, the walls are hung with red velvet. 6. Painted room signed 'Nicolas Piemont'.

4

5

6

The Louis XIV style adapted to Dutch taste continued up till the 1740's.
1. The dining room of the Huis ten Bosch was designed by Daniel Marot and illustrates his last phase (1735). The grisaille painting over the chimneypiece is by Jacob de Wit.
2. Stucco ceiling of the same room.
3. Chimneypiece of carved wood from the province of Groningen decorated with a painting by J. A. Wassenbergh, dated 1741.

The French influence

2   3

1. Angle of a panelled room painted in green and gilded. Marble chimneypiece with overmantel of mirror in carved wood frame. The high-backed chairs date, like the room, from about 1720; the oak table is 17th century.
2. Chimneypiece from a house in Delft.
3. Reconstruction of a chimneypiece from a house in Utrecht. The plaster relief of Pluto and Persephone is cast from a marble original.
4. Staircase of a house in the Kaisersgraacht in Amsterdam with carved wood balustrade in the Louis XIV style. The walls are decorated with plaster figures in niches.

217

1

3

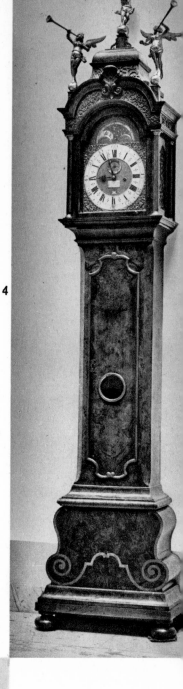

4

2

5

The English influence

1. Walnut settee in green silk with panels of *petit-point*.
2, 3. From the beginning of the 18th century the English influence on Dutch furniture appears in chairs with high curved backs. In (3) the back and apron have marquetry decoration, the feet terminate in the 'claw and ball' motif.
4, 5. Long-case clocks in walnut surmounted by gilt bronze figures of Fame and Time. The latter signed by A. van Oostrom, Amsterdam.

1. Commode veneered in root walnut. The design dating from about 1720 is typically Dutch.
2. This bureau-bookcase with star inlay is English in outline.
3. Another bureau-bookcase, in walnut. The two volutes recalling Dutch chimneypieces of the period conceal a number of small drawers.
4. Table commode of about 1730 with original marquetry.

2 3

4

1. Cabinet veneered in root walnut; the doors and sides are decorated with *petit-point* panels.

2, 3. China cabinets; veneered in walnut. The great quantity of Chinese porcelain imported into Holland in the 17th century gave rise to these cabinets which were often to be found in the rich burgher homes. The wall behind the cabinet (3) is hung with a verdure tapestry from the factory of A. Baert of Amsterdam.

2

3

Dutch Rococo

1. Armchair and commode about 1730. 2. Armchair and footstool of carved and gilded wood covered in green velvet. On the back the arms of Orange-Nassau. This was used by the Stadtholder at the Admiralty in Amsterdam. Executed by N. Bruynestein in 1748. 3. Armchair in painted and gilded wood covered in green velvet. This chair, which is directly inspired by Louis XV designs, was used by the Stadtholder William V when on a visit to Amsterdam in 1768. 4, 5. Armchair and chair in mahogany upholstered in red velvet. The chair is a happy blend of English and French influences.

1

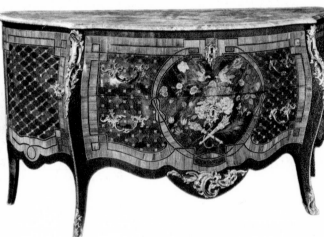

3

2

1. Angle of a room, reconstructed in the Museum of Utrecht. The walls are hung in red Utrecht velvet. The white and gold chairs depend on French models. The showcase at the back contains Dutch porcelain.

2. A finely designed mahogany tea-table. By the middle of the 18th century mahogany was in frequent use.

3. Marquetry commode of about 1760 in in which the French influence is manifest.

4

5

6

7

4. Wardrobe of veneered walnut, about 1750.

5. Bureau-bookcase with mirror doors; on the angles, a barometer and thermometer dated 1754. The desk front is inlaid with a monogram in marquetry.

6. Cabinet veneered in walnut. The mirror doors are decorated with Japanese subjects in *verre églomisé*; enrichments of floral marquetry and silver escutcheons.

7. Corner cabinet dating from about 1750. The root walnut veneer is of exceptional quality.

1, 2. Staircase with mahogany balustrade from a house in the Kaisersgraacht, Amsterdam (1748). 3. Chimneypiece of about 1760; the overmantel painted in green and gilded. 4. Chimneypiece from the Chinese Room at the Royal Palace of the Huis ten Bosch, near The Hague. The marble surround dates from 1735, the overmantel, painted in black and gold, dates from about 1770.

Opposite page: Salon of 1748 from a house in the Kaisersgraacht, Amsterdam. The surround is of marble; the overmantel is of richly carved mahogany, enclosing a painting by Jacob de Wit.
On the right is a cabinet covered in *petit-point* on an early 18th-century stand in the Chinese taste.

Classicism

From the Royal Palace of the Huis ten Bosch near The Hague:

1. The Green Saloon hung with green damask. The carved and gilded Louis XVI chairs are covered in damask of the same colour; on the walls are family portraits.

2. The Blue Saloon. The walls are hung with damask to blend with the grey and gold French furniture.

3. Painted and gilded Louis XVI Salon from a house in Utrecht. The walls are hung with silk woven with figures of Hercules. The chairs in front of the windows are painted in grey and white.

2

1

3

1. Secretaire with marquetry decoration on a satin-wood ground, each panel inset with a medallion of Chinese lacquer on a black ground. The handles of the top drawer are enamelled.

2. Commode-side-table with marquetry decoration on a satinwood ground. The top rises to disclose racks for glass and china and a pewter container for washing up.

3, 4. Two further examples, one with columnettes at the corners, the caps and bases of metal, the other ornamented with classical scenes painted *en camieu* on a blue ground.

1

2

3

1. Chamber organ in mahogany, bearing the stamp of H. H. Hess, Gouda, and the date 1792.
2. Cupboard with lozenge decoration in marquetry. This piece was probably originally designed as a bookcase with brass lattice-work over the panels.
3. Cupboard in carved mahogany enclosing drawers intended for a natural history collection.

229

1

2

3

1. Salon in the French taste with painted panels by A. van Stry from a house in Dordrecht.
2. Dining room from the Huis ten Donck near Rotterdam. The classical chimneypiece contains a painted panel.
3. Angle of a room designed by the architect Abraham van der Hart about 1790. The panelling painted in blue, grey, light green and white comes from a house in Haarlem. The chairs, carpet and chandelier were designed for the room.
4. Panels of painted landscape were a popular decoration in the 18th century. This fine example is drawn from a house in Amsterdam. It was painted by Jurriaan Andriessen (1776).

4

Louis Bonaparte

Changes of style are generally preceded by a period of transition. In times of peace these usually witness the creation of hybrid works and decorative ideas drawn from earlier periods. It is otherwise when the new forms follow in the train of war.

Indeed, the contrast may be marked, as in this example from a house in Amsterdam. The panels are still in the 18th-century tradition, although executed at the opening of the 19th century, but the furnishings are in a pure Louis Bonaparte (King of Holland, 1806-1810) taste. The gilt bronze table-centre is by Thomire.

Louis Bonaparte encouraged the development of an Empire style by lavish commissions. He refurnished the entire Royal Palace at Amsterdam.

1. Cylinder top desk of Louis Bonaparte in mahogany and gilt bronze made by Carel Breytspraak (1808) for the King's bedroom.

2. Armchair in mahogany and gilt bronze by Joseph Cuel (1809). This chair, originally covered in white and yellow silk, came from the bedroom of Queen Hortense.

3, 4. Empire side-cupboard, side-table and work-table.

1

3

4

233

1

2

Eclecticism

4

1. Bureau cabinet in mahogany with neo-gothic decoration of about 1840. Inside, a display of contemporary silhouettes and objects.
2, 3. Mid-19th-century room: the furniture of mahogany upholstered in tapestry with fringes and applied work. On the walls, contemporary portraits.
4. Tea-table with a tapestry cover of the period and lacquered metal kettle and stand.

3

1

2

Modernism

The first manifestations of the new trends in architecture and decoration became apparent in Holland at the end of the last century. The architect H. P. Berlage was one of the leading pioneers of the movement which was to influence the whole of Europe.

1, 2. Room designed by L. Cachet from a house in Amsterdam. The overmantel is in faïence.

3. A collector's cabinet designed by the same artist.

3

3

1 2

4

Indonesian furniture

Indonesian furniture in the 17th century came under strong Dutch influence, while retaining its native taste for elaborate decoration.

1, 2. This table, coffer, chair and plate rack afford typical examples of the style.

3. Chair in ironwood, the design of which follows close upon Dutch models. From the Coromandel Coast.

4. A cabinet and chair in ebony decorated with foliage scrolls in relief, representative of the Jakarta workshops.

THE LIVING TRADITION

1 2

3

The Castle of Popta

1. The 'Heringa State' at Marssum in Friesland was built in the 16th century and restored in 1631. In 1687 it was acquired by Dr Henricus Popta, a lawyer of Leeuwarden, who added a home for poor women.
2. Gateway opening on to the courtyard.
3. Entrance to the house at the base of the West Tower.

1 2

3　4

5

The 'Heringa State' is the only well-preserved old manor house in South Holland. It was carefully restored at the beginning of this century, and contains a number of fine rooms.

1. Stone chimneypiece in the Great Hall dating from 1631. The supporting figures represent Fidelity and Truth.

2. Stone doorway with figures of Religion and Hope. The oak door bears the arms of Tjalling van Eysinga and his wife Eets van Hiddema.

3. General view of the same room. The cabinet and draw-end table date from the 17th century.

4. Base of the spiral staircase.

5. A corridor serves as entrance hall and gives access to the rooms through the fine doorway of brick and carved stone.

1

4

1, 2. Two beds built into recesses in the panelling. The first dates from around 1630.

3. 18th-century folding table of painted wood from Hindelopen with a traditional rush chair.

4. Chimneypiece from an anteroom at the 'Heringa State', dating from about 1630. The oak mantelshelf is supported on stone half-columns; the surround is of Delft tiles.

2

3

A burgher's house from The Hague

In general, Dutch houses have steep and narrow stairs, though this does not always preclude an elaborate decoration, as is shown (1) in the newel post.

2. A small Zeeland cupboard of oak inlaid with various woods and some early woodwork.

3. Another view. The chair dates from the 18th century; the display-cabinet contains some fine examples of Delft faïence.

1

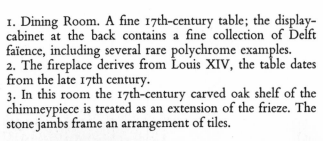

1. Dining Room. A fine 17th-century table; the display-cabinet at the back contains a fine collection of Delft faïence, including several rare polychrome examples.

2. The fireplace derives from Louis XIV, the table dates from the late 17th century.

3. In this room the 17th-century carved oak shelf of the chimneypiece is treated as an extension of the frieze. The stone jambs frame an arrangement of tiles.

2   3

1

The general arrangement of this 18th-century house at The Hague recalls that of many town houses built by wealthy burghers at the same time or during the previous century, such as we find in the Herengraacht, Kaisersgraacht or the Prinzensgraacht at Amsterdam. The canal front is frequently surmounted by a pediment. Passing through the house, we often find a small garden such as this (1), with lawns with box edging and the traditional sundial surrounded by flowers and shrubs.

2. At the end of the garden, a charmingly designed pavilion.

3. In the hall a 17th-century oak table is flanked by two 18th-century walnut chairs of about 1720. The Flemish tapestry dates from the end of the 17th century.

A notable 18th-century house on a canal

2

3

1

1. Large carved oak cupboard from Friesland. 2, 3. Two views of the main salon. The white and gold doors and chimneybreast are in the Louis XIV taste. On the walls, an 18th-century tapestry, decorative paintings and two mirror wall lights of a later date.

2

3

1

2

1. In this small, intimate room the walls are stretched with Utrecht velvet. The pictures date from the 17th century. Opposite the chimneypiece stands a large bureau-bookcase (2) surmounted by Delft vases.

245

1

2

Village houses from the Zaan

1. A group of 18th-century green and white painted houses from the Zaan district, re-erected in the open-air Museum at Arnhem.

2, 3, 4. The so-called 'pronkkammer'—the best room—would be reserved for formal occasions such as weddings and funerals. The built-in cupboard houses a choice collection of silver and porcelain. The larger of the painted corner cabinets, showing a scene of the Prodigal Son, is dated 1798. The oak chair by the fireplace is dated 1777. The three chairs and table with the Bible are of painted wood.

1. The bureau in this green and white painted room dates from the 18th century. The hanging clock is local work.
2. Light brownish-mauve painted bedroom. The painted oval table and rush chairs date from the early 19th century.
3. A so-called 'Zaankamer' or 'Luchthuis' in which the family would congregate on Sundays to watch the river. The wooden ceiling is treated like the cabin of a boat. The folding wooden table is painted with landscape medallions on a flecked ground matching the chairs.

1

2

3

SPAIN

Introduction

Any special characteristics which may distinguish Spain from the rest of Europe are due in large part to the fact that it was for centuries the bastion against Islam. In 711 the Moors crossed the Straits of Gibraltar. They remained in the Peninsula until 1498.

These eight hundred years of Moslem occupation were in the main a period of wars, of conquests and defeats. Yet in the intervals of respite culture and crafts intermingled and developed. In the same year as the discovery of America, King Boabdil capitulated to the Catholic throne and a new era dawned.

The luxury of the Moorish courts, the Caliphate of Cordoba, the kingdoms of Granada and Seville astounded the Spaniards. The meeting of these two worlds gave rise to the *mudéjar* style. Here oriental craftsmanship and techniques reappear in the inlaid work, the use of precious materials and leatherwork, particularly at Cordoba; and the intricate geometrical forms of stars and interlaced work are found on elaborate doors and ceilings. Some social customs also persisted, such as that by which women sat on cushions on the floor.

Frontispiece
The Infanta Maria-Theresa of Spain

by Juan Bautista del Mazo.

This, then, was the background to the Spanish Renaissance. The advent of the Hapsburgs tightened the associations with Europe. Together with a predilection for Italian art, the Emperor Charles V also introduced elements of German discipline, which his son, Philip II, adapted and translated to a Spanish idiom.

Under Philip IV the Flemish wars brought about yet closer exchanges which were to culminate, by the 17th century, in the great period of Spanish painting, sculpture and decorative arts.

When the building of the Armada stripped the forests, pine became the most popular material. From this wood, painted and gilded, the elaborate Baroque furnishings were produced under Philip V, and brought to the Court of Madrid something of the luxury and extravagance of Versailles.

Later, in the 18th century, Charles III set up the Royal Factories for tapestry and porcelains. Decoration in the oriental taste, drawing its inspiration largely from the Philippines, enjoyed some vogue.

In addition to Court influences, the upper classes drew upon English sources and both 'Queen Anne' and 'Chippendale' styles played some part. Under Charles IV and Ferdinand VII the decorative arts tended to follow in the general European wake and no very significant contributions were made—apart, perhaps, from regional developments in Majorca, Catalonia or Valencia, where a certain delicacy of treatment offers some pleasant additions to European furniture of the 19th century.

But if these movements affected the decoration of the great palaces and the houses of the rich, art in the provinces remained and still remains true to the old traditions.

M. L. SOUGEZ

1

2

Gothic

1. This fine Toledo ceiling of painted interlacing heightened in gold is a typical example of *mudéjar* art, that is to say, of a Christian interpretation of a Mohammedan technique as opposed to 'mozarabic' or 'hispano-mauresque', which are terms applied to Mohammedan works produced in the Peninsula.

2. Another 16th-century Toledan ceiling from the Palace of Fuensalida, while *mudéjar* in decoration, is European in its construction and exposed beams.

3. A rare cupboard of the late 15th century with four doors with linenfold panels and armorial painting. The fine mounts and hinges are of wrought iron.

4. Sacristy coffer-bench of the same period, also with linenfold panels.

3

4

1

2   3

Charles V

1. Bench of simple construction in which the back hinges on to the seat. It is richly carved in the Renaissance style with a battle scene and coat-of-arms.

2. Armchair of *mudéjar* design with floral decoration inlaid in light wood and bone.

3. Table and small cabinet of drawers. A charming example of *mudéjar* work inlaid with coloured woods. The low treatment probably implies that it was designed for a woman—rather than a child—since it was still the custom, inherited from Islam, for the women to receive in rooms surrounded by a low platform covered with cushions and with low furnishings. The practice persisted into the 17th century.

1

2

3

The 'bargueño', or nest of drawers designed to stand on a table, was the Spanish variant of the cabinet. 1, 2. Fine examples in gilded wood dating from the 16th century. The name derives from the village of Vargas or Bargas, in the province of Toledo, where such pieces were produced.

3. A bargueño closed. Here the decoration is limited to the wrought ironwork applied to the plain wood surface. The table stand is typical for such pieces, the two mask heads serve as handles for the slide which draws out to support the fall front.

4. Fine Renaissance table in which the elaborate carving stands out against the simple overall design. The iron stretchers were designed to keep clothing from touching the brazier beneath.

Opposite page: Fine Renaissance bed showing Italian influence. The spiral columns support a frieze of cherub heads. The decorations are in gilt wood and metal. A votive lamp hangs from the exposed beams of the Toledo ceiling.

4

Philip II

Under Philip II, the Hapsburg dynasty really becomes dominant in the Peninsula. The Renaissance style introduced by the Emperor Charles V takes on a severer form.

1. A 'frailero', a square hard seat adapted from church or monastery furniture.
2. Typical example of a seat with hinged back; the hinges form the sole decoration. The metal leg stays recall folding furniture.
3, 4. Two other benches, somewhat archaic in design, though with carved backs contrasting with the simple peasant legs.

1

2

3

4

257

1 2

3

4

5

6

1, 3. Two coffers, often called 'marriage coffers', from Catalonia, though of Italian inspiration. These served for keeping clothes. The first depends upon the play of woods for its decorative effect, the second is carved, including the inside of the lid. Both are typically architectural in treatment.

2. A credence with four doors which is Portuguese in origin or inspiration. At the time Portugal was allied to the Spanish crown. The reversed scrolls and heavy legs are noteworthy.

4. A bargueño, again influenced by architectural design, dating from the late 16th century. The supporting table is a provincial piece of the 17th century.

5. Early 17th-century bargueño and stand with simple inlaid ornament.

6. Bargueño and matching stand of the late 16th century with geometrical decoration. Such pieces herald the later cupboards and buffets.

1

2

3

4

1

2

Opposite page: 1. Wood doorway with interlaced geometric ornament derived from Moorish sources.

2. Peasant table with drawers decorated with rosettes inlaid with bone, and two chairs with turned splats—a long-favoured decoration, particularly in Andalusia.

3. Profusely ornamented provincial cupboard.

4. Pine cupboard of the second half of the 16th century with a traditional provincial decoration of different-sized rectangles known as *cuarterones*.

This page: 1. Dining room in a Toledan palace with its noticeably severe furnishings: upright chairs and plain-topped table, only the feet of which have any decoration.

2. Another view. The brazier with pointed top is of a type still found in Estramadura.

1   2

1. Fine 16th-century interior. The frailero armchair is
upholstered in brocade, the front stretcher is elaborately
carved though the arms are plain. The carved foliage on
the drawers forms the sole ornament of the table.
2. Tester bed covered in velvet and green and gold
brocade; the light is of wrought iron.

1. An ensemble of 16th- and 17th-century furniture. The panels of the late 16th-century coffer are enclosed in heavy carved framework.
2. Provincial kitchen with local pottery from Toledo and Valencia, and ironwork from Estramadura.
3. Fine mid-16th-century refectory table. The seats are upholstered in velvet worked in gold and silver.

1

2

3

1

1. The decoration on this fine table is rather simpler and more provincial than the example on the previous page. 2. Small fruitwood chair of a type that has persisted until the present time in provincial areas. 3. Coffer chest in black stained wood, provincial chairs and metal plates surrounding an elaborate mirror.

2

3

Opposite page: This setting in a Toledo palace recalls that of a great Spanish house of the 17th century. The writing chair, copper brazier, stool and coffer stand harmoniously against the white walls and El Greco painting.

1

2

3

4

Philip IV

5

Four chairs belonging to the same period, differing considerably in design and quality of material.
1. Provincial seat with drawer base. Andalusian work, probably from the region of Granada.
2. Bench with hinged back and velvet-covered sacristy chair.
3. Chair covered in leather held by large bronze nails.
4. Provincial version of the stiff frailero armchair.
5. Rush-seated armchair with diamond cut ornament typical of Andalusian work.

1, 2. The decoration of brass-headed nails on these two leather coffers embraces the owners' names on the lid. The second rests on a stand ornamented to match; the locks and hinges form an integral part of the decoration.
3. Fine 17th-century bar*gueño* probably from Aragon. The *mudéjar* tradition is manifest in the six little panels inlaid with bone.
4. Small coffer combining Renaissance heads with traditional geometric ornament.

Several examples of bargueños of the second half of the 16th century.

1. Inlaid with engraved ivory and tortoiseshell. The Italian influence is strongly marked, especially in the small central architectural motif.

2. Similar Italian influences are to be found in the elaborate carving, the central statuette and surmounting balustrade as well as in the bronze appliques and tortoiseshell.

3, 4. In contrast, the restraint of these two examples betrays their Spanish origin. The upper parts are provided with handles for easy lifting. The decoration is limited to marquetry, in one case showing the basque swastika. The stands are provincial.

5. Bargueño in gilded wood. The stand, 'taquillon', is separate though apparently part of the whole. The gilded Catalan chairs are later.

3

1

4

5

2

1. Desk of the second half of the 17th century. The lower part consists of drawers, the upper has a sloping fall front. 2. Movable jalousie from a 17th-century palace reminiscent of Moorish work. 3. Provincial cupboard of the 17th century, the lower part with decoration of *cuarterones* enclosing a cross at the centre. The star pattern jalousie doors of the upper part derive from *mudéjar*; they are surmounted by a cornice worthy of any 18th-century European furniture. 4. Provincial cupboard in light walnut; the design of the panel ornaments conforms with the architectural traditions of the 18th century. The provincial chair is probably basque.

5. Large cupboard; the elaboration of treatment and material as well as the craftsmanship suggest Italian influence. 6. A provincial 17th-century cupboard interesting for the development of this type of furniture, the lower part with two tiers of carved panels recalling the taquillon stands for bargueños. The second stage has openwork bars. The third completes the proportions of the high cupboard. 7. Carved pine cupboard manifestly indebted to *mudéjar* tradition. The wrought iron handles are attached to plaques of cut sheet-iron.

5

6   7

1. A group of provincial Catalan furniture of the 17th century.

2. 17th-century bed of turned wood decorated with bronze-headed nails: a bronze *Ecce Homo* is inset at the top. From Estramadura.

3. Iron tester bed with primitive religious painting in the iron medallion at the head. Hangings of traditional Toledo work in red and black on a white ground.

4. Majorcan bed-head of the 17th century in turned wood; inset, a bronze medallion of the *Nativity*.

5. 17th-century bed from Salamanca shows the neighbouring Portuguese influence. The wood here is almost entirely covered in bronze sheeting.

2

1

3

1

3

2

1. Provincial kitchen of the 17th century: the walls at the back of the vast fireplace are covered with tiled decoration (*azulejos*), while the mantelpiece is decorated with a splendid collection of ceramics from the region of Teruel.

2. Detail of the same kitchen: worthy of note are the utensils of wood and wrought iron, a child's high chair and the peasant chest with decorations resembling provincial embroidery, and bearing the inscription '*Viva Maria Hernandez*'.

3. Suite of traditional furniture of the 17th century, table with carved legs, stiff chairs covered with brocade. The hand-made rug, provincial work from Andalusia, covers a red brick floor inset with multi-coloured tiles.

Philip V

1. An interesting Catalan bed in wood painted green and gold; from the beginning of the 18th century. A typical example of furniture from the village of Olot, in the region of Gerona, which is famous for polychrome and gilded pieces.
2. This bed shows the same characteristics, though with less elegant lines and less gilding; the headboard is inset with a painting.
3. Door with rich carving and marquetry work.

1

2

3

1. Although this chair is purely Iberian in material and treatment, with its repoussé leather and nails, the form owes much to Europe.

2. The bright painting and French outline of this Spanish 18th-century table is in marked contrast to the severity of earlier periods. The vases in cut and painted sheet metal are typical of altar furniture.

3. This Catalan chair with carved and gilt enrichments is based on contemporary English design.

4. Bench in carved and painted wood in the Portuguese taste dating from the reign of Ferdinand IV.

1

2

3

4

Charles III

1. A provincial Andalusian piece. It is independent of its stand like the earlier bargueño, and is similarly furnished with handles for easy transport.
2. Provincial side-table of the 18th century based on English and French designs.
3. Table painted with *chinoiserie* motifs. Provincial chairs with esparto grass seats; the type has persisted down to present day in Catalonia, Valencia and Andalusia.

1

2 3

1

2

3

1. Catalan bed from Olot (province of Gerona) in green and gold painted wood, adapted from a Louis XV model.

2. Catalan long-case clock in painted wood. The general form persists through to the end of the 19th century.

3. Painted 18th-century cupboard. A happy adaptation of a traditional Spanish design with panelled doors to the lower part and jalousies above. The marquetry chairs manifestly owe a great deal to general 18th-century European forms. The corner cupboard is painted and gilded.

Opposite page: Rococo bedroom in painted wood. 1. Showcase with grille doors. The shelves over the chairs are designed to take plates, with cups and pots hung below.

2. Bed with richly-painted head. Such painted furniture was very popular along the Mediterranean litoral (Catalonia and Valencia).

1

2

1. Corner console in red painted wood; the gilded carving shows French influence. 2. Marbled showcase with gilded carving. The flanking processional lanterns have multi-coloured glass. 3, 4. An unusual piece in fruitwood, shown closed and open. Designed like a bureau-bookcase it opens to disclose a small oratory. The drawers are for vestments, and the small drawers to take the mass candlesticks. The upper section with its crucifix serves as an altar.

Charles IV

1. A quiet, elegant, caned seat, with restrained gilt-bronze mounts.
2. Side-table with column and lyre supports with gilt-bronze mounts. Many variants of such pieces were produced in Spain during the 19th century for the display of objects such as decorated the chimneypiece in France. Such 'French' chimneypieces failed to supplant the traditional Spanish brazier.

1

3

2

4

3. A console table, mirror and seats in the Louis XVI style, all based upon French designs, even down to the silk used for the upholstery. The Valencian silk weavers sought to rival those of Lyons.
4. Further examples of French influence are to be noted in the porcelain mirror and appliques from the Royal factory of Buen Retiro, Madrid, founded by Charles III.

1

2

1. Mahogany cabinet with ormolu mounts
in the Empire taste. The clock is English.
The chair is part of a suite.
2. The suite includes this seat. All are of
mahogany with gilded wood decoration of
arrows and stars. The plaques with mythological subjects on the back rail are painted
in gold and black under glass.

1

2

3

Two extreme but amusing examples of provincial decorative art are to be found in these kitchens with tiled walls from the region of Valencia.

The example illustrated in 1, 2 and 3 is in its original state. St Anthony watches over the cooking, while almost life-size figures are engaged in the daily chores against the background of cooking implements and hams and sausages (2 and 3).

4. and *opposite page:* Exact reconstruction of a period kitchen. The objects painted on the tiles mingle with actual objects. The tile stone is ancestor of the type still to be found on terraces adjoining kitchens. The room here is under the protection of Our Lady of Carmel.

4

Ferdinand VII

2

3

4

1. The drapery with fringes and pompoms is painted in *trompe l'œil*. The style was popular above all in Madrid.

2. Mahogany console with rather heavy decoration. The light, practical chairs which owe much to English design were almost exclusively produced in Majorca, or occasionally on the neighbouring mainland of Valencia and Catalonia.

3. A group of chairs typical of the design of the period of Ferdinand VII. Special feature is the small cylindrical bolster with wood ends. The legs with their combination of lion feet and eagle wings offer a curious compromise.

4. A salon of the period. The rather heavy sofa is inlaid. The neo-gothic occasional table is rather later.

1

2

1. This large dressing-mirror owes much to Empire design, but the heavy ormolu and marquetry points to the Restoration. The cornucopias support small drum-shaped drawers.

2. Marquetry console with lyre supports; the feather and flower decoration of the front is unusual.

3. Console mirror with decoration in marquetry and gilded wood.

4. Slightly less carving and more marquetry feature in this dressing-table. All these pieces owe much to foreign influences, though adapted to local traditions. The craftsmanship is notable even if the line may leave something to be desired.

5. A rather more restrained group in the Ferdinand style. The portrait of the future Queen Isabella gives a somewhat intimate bourgeois tone to the room.

1

Three Spanish table pianos. 1. In burr-ash, harmonises with the neo-classical chairs and painting.
2. A more restrained example.
3. Signed 'J. Colmenejero, Madrid', and dated 1827. The interior has delicate marquetry work.

2   3

1 2

3

Three variants of beds from the Peninsula. 1. The head with swan and eagle decoration is based on Empire design, but the more elaborate inlay of the foot points to Restoration.
2. Probably originating in Majorca, this example shows English influence.
3. This boat-shaped bed is of simpler design, while the chair is very elaborate. The blind painted in flowers was popular at the time.

Isabella

1. Neo-gothic occasional table deriving immediately from architectural sources. 2. Surprising throne armchair in gilded wood upholstered in crimson velvet with footstool *en suite*. 3. A 'romantic' corner. A painted wood console and Madrid chairs covered in multi-coloured embroideries of birds, butterflies and so on from the Philippines. The fringes recall those of the well-known Manilla shrawls.

Opposite page: 4. Dining room with painted *trompe l'œil* decoration on the ceiling; the drapery is emblazoned with the arms of the provinces of Spain. The pedestal table divides to allow for leaf extension. The chairs have marquetry decoration. The secretary-bookcase, called a 'chinero', recalls the traditional Catalan 'canteranos'. Such pieces served many uses, such as cupboard, dresser, book-case, cabinet. Variations influenced by English taste are found in the Balearics.

2   3

1. In this Isabella room the medallion-shaped back of the chairs is repeated in the sofa. The furniture is arranged round the brazier.
2. A 'romantic' dressing table, recalling Empire design in the column legs and drawers, and with neo-gothic elements in the mirror supports.
3. Detail of a 'romantic' room. The dressing table again shows Empire elements in the mounts and simplicity of line. In the corner a mirror on stand, sometimes termed a 'page'.

Opposite page: 1. Typical room of the period of Isabella II. The curtains match the upholstery of the furniture arranged round a gilt brass brazier. The carpet from the Royal Manufactory at Madrid of about 1850.
2. Another view of the 'romantic' room (3), with a bed of the Isabella period, the head ornamented with a marquetry panel of doves. On the left, a small mahogany oratory from Catalonia or Majorca.

1

2   3

4

5

Alfonzo

1

2

3

1. Majorcan chest with pewter inlay. This type of furniture came in at the Romantic period and is characteristic of the workshops of the Mediterranean coast (Catalonia and the Balearics).
2. Room with plush and lace upholstery; the period made lavish use of pompoms, heavy raised embroidery and rich galon, especially developed in the Americas and Philippines.
3. Furniture in black wood with painting and mother-of-pearl inlay, analogous to French taste under Napoleon III.

THE LIVING TRADITION

1

2

A house near Madrid

1. A modern house in the traditional style. Original wood jalousies, wrought iron grilles and reliefs collected from various parts—mainly Castile—serve to decorate the brick façade.

2. Passage between the dining room and salon with jalousie doorway. To the right an agreeable provincial 17th-century piece, and above it a painted mirror. The fine 18th-century door is executed in two contrasting woods, and pieces of 17th- and 18th-century painted carving from altars are placed over the doors and windows.

3. Detail of first floor corridor. The modern doors are decorated with panels inspired by traditional *cuarterones*.

4. Old shutters have been placed on the windows, and below, a 17th-century church bench. At the small table—a 'tocinera' (probably originally designed for cutting bacon)—stands a frailero upholstered in embroidered velvet. On the wall a carved and painted wood framed mirror, in the niche a polychrome bust of Christ.

5. The door opening from the hall on to the terrace comes from a convent at Toledo.

3

4

5

Three views of the dining room: 1. 17th- and 18th-century silver decorates the massive table. The 'frailero' chair is upholstered in embroidered green velvet.
2. A Baroque mirror hangs over the small-panelled double doors of the wall cupboard.
3. Under the window is a table with folding top. A vine twines among the wrought iron bars of the grille.

1

3

A Madrid apartment

2

1. The anteroom walls are stretched with raw silk with gold thread. An 18th-century Dutch chair and wrought iron lampstand accompany the 17th-century cupboard doors painted in black and gold. A contemporary idiom is emphasized in this salon (3), as elsewhere in the apartment: the ironwork chairs have leather seats, the sofa and pictures are framed with simple moulding, while to the right stand two bamboo trunks. At the same time, a traditional Spanish element is maintained by some antique pieces, such as the large six-leg table and the leather-covered chair (2).

Two views of the salon: 1. The fireplace is flanked by carved wooden beams; on the wall a polychrome angel and two Baroque panels. 2. A provincial table and ironwork grille stand by the modern sofa; to the right is a marquetry desk in the *mudéjar* tradition, dated 1646.

1

2 3

3. The dining room is furnished with Dutch chairs round a folding Spanish table in natural pine; above the modern console a still-life by Augustin Hernandez.

A collector's home

1. On either side of the door opening on to the hall stand a Baroque lectern, a chair and an openwork screen of Goan work, against a background of books.

2. The desk of the owner (who is a well-known writer) is a fine 17th-century piece; the benches and small tables of the same period display a collection of manuscripts, books, statuettes and minerals, giving personality and life to this spacious room.

1

2

1

1. In the dining room is a Portuguese chest of the period of João V; above, a Valencian wall cabinet, called a 'vasar', with marquetry decoration and gilded wood carving.

2. Sideboard made from a part of a polychrome Baroque altar set out with a collection of ceramics and silver. The chairs derive from English models.

2

3

4

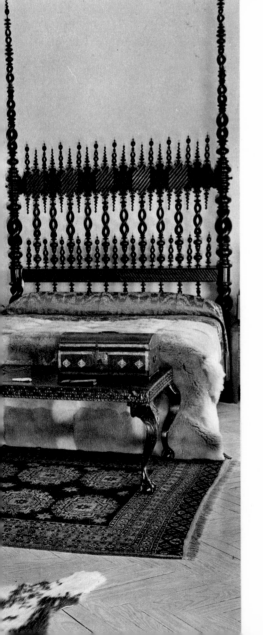

The master bedroom. 3. Portuguese bed of 'Bilros' style, silver candelabra; at the foot of the bed a Portuguese table of the time of João V, like the chest.

4. On the wall a *Virgin* of the school of Zurbarán. The curtain ties and pelmets are made from strips of red velvet embroidered with gold of the 17th century.

5. The wall facing the bed is hung with a collection of provincial *en votos*, over the fireplace which can be closed by painted doors. To the left, a 17th-century coffer.

5

In an old palace

1. The main staircase has been restored to its original dignity. The stone lion, painted wood seat, wall brackets with metal holders and typical Spanish armorial hangings (*repostero*) enhance the marbled walls. A long gallery is partitioned by furniture to serve as entrance hall and lounge.

2. A general view of the hall, with an old church doorway with *cuartarones* leading to the study. It is flanked by an ingenious stand of wrought iron with adjustable glass shelves (3), displaying a group of barber's dishes in copper, pewter and pottery.

Opposite page: 4. On the other side of the hall from the stand (3), a boxwood statuette of St James stands on a 17th-century table accompanied by a chair of the same period.

5. A white-painted jalousie serves to divide this very large room. Old black and white Andalusian embroidered bed-covers are used as mats.

3

5

4

Two views of the salon: 1. Provincial 17th-century cedarwood table with pewter candlesticks. The 18th-century mirrors above the sofa flank a modern painting.

2. The low table in front of the yellow marble fireplace is made from a round sheet of glass resting on a brazier.

Opposite page: The velvet-covered bed is flanked by two tables of the period of Philip V. Two Baroque columns are placed against the moiré walls.